The Canadian
Snowbird in
America

Professional Tax and Financial Insights into
Temporary Lifestyles in the U.S.

TERRY F. RITCHIE, with Brian D. Wruk

Published by ECW PRESS
2120 Queen Street East, Suite 200, Toronto, Ontario, Canada M4E 1E2

LIBRARY AND ARCHIVES CANADA CATALOGUING IN PUBLICATION

Ritchie, Terry F.
The Canadian snowbird in America : professional tax and financial insights into temporary lifestyles in the U.S. / Terry F. Ritchie with Brian D. Wruk.

ISBN 978-1-55022-804-5

1. Canadians—United States—Finance, Personal. 2. Canadians—Taxation—Law and legislation—United States. 3. Canadians—Legal status, laws, etc.—United States. 4. Canadians—Retirement—United States. I. Wruk, Brian D. II. Title.

HG179.R58 2007   332.024008911073   C2007-903570-1

Text Design: Tania Craan
Cover Image: Miguel S. Salmeron and Charles McRae
Typesetting: Mary Bowness
Production: Rachel Brooks
Printing: Thomson-Shore

This book is set in Minion and Franklin Gothic

The publication of *The Canadian Snowbird in America* has been generously supported by the Government of Canada through the Book Publishing Industry Development Program.

Canadä

DISTRIBUTION
CANADA: Jaguar Book Group, 100 Armstrong Ave., Georgetown, ON L7G 5S4
UNITED STATES: Independent Publishers Group, 814 North Franklin Street, Chicago, Illinois 60610

PRINTED AND BOUND IN THE UNITED STATES

DISCLAIMER
This book presents information of a general nature and is not intended to be an opinion on any specific individual situation. The book also contains legal and tax information that should not be construed as providing legal or tax advice. While the authors have endeavored to ensure the book's accuracy and timeliness, no one should act upon it without appropriate professional advice after a thorough examination of the facts of a particular situation. Readers are encouraged to seek the assistance of qualified legal and tax professionals regarding their own specific situation.

ECW PRESS
ecwpress.com

Table of Contents

V. Till Death Do Us Part: U.S. Estate Planning Issues for Snowbirds 89

I dedicate this book to my late twin sister Sherri.
Thank you for showing me the way.

Preface

Quietly Gord awoke. He wanted to make sure that Shirley had a few extra hours of sleep. Today was the day they were to make their annual trek down south. It usually took about three days, and Gord was hoping that with a few extra hours of sleep, Shirley would be able to help with the driving. He was hopeful that this year they could make it in two days.

Every year about this time for the past six years, Gord and Shirley have "spread their wings" and flown down to the Scottsdale, Arizona, area. Well, actually, they'd just get in their new Dodge Caravan and drive down to Arizona. However, to their friends and neighbors, they were "snowbirds" flying south for the winter. They knew that many of their friends and neighbors were kind of envious of their annual migration.

Gord and Shirley always had their act together. It was a way of life for them, a life they enjoyed and looked forward to. In fact, Gord had become somewhat of an expert on many of the issues that Canadian snowbirds face when going to the United States.

They had developed a budget, and they knew — to the penny — what they could and could not do while down in Arizona. Each year they prayed that the "loonie," named after the diving — yes, diving — bird that floats carefree on the face of the Canadian dollar coin, would rebound, and finally their prayers had been answered. "The way things are going," Gord suggested, "this thing could be at par by Christmas!" Given the number of winters they'd been in the United States, they knew too well the impact that a fluctuating loonie can have on the snowbird lifestyle.

With their past winter experiences behind them, Gord and Shirley had become more aware of the financial, health, and tax consequences of spending time in the United States. In fact, this year Gord suggested to Shirley that they take six of those large 24-roll packages of toilet paper with them instead of the four they'd taken in previous years. "Great idea, that should last us," Shirley replied.

❋ ❋ ❋

Having practiced in the areas of Canada-U.S. financial, tax, and estate planning for over 20 years, I've had the occasion to meet and work with many snowbirds from all across Canada. However, I haven't been able to find a comprehensive resource that truly addresses their unique needs. My partner, Brian Wruk, and I are hopeful that this book is such a resource.

Given the complex and ever-changing Canada-U.S. immigration, income tax, and estate tax rules, we are unashamed to say we don't know everything! To that end, we have been fortunate to have built a large network of trusted and competent allied professionals to work with us. We have drawn upon some of those experts to review various parts of this book and want to thank them individually for their assistance in making a book like this possible.

Richard Brunton, CA, CPA, of the Brunton-McCarthy firm of Boca Raton, Florida, is the old — or shall we say "mature" — guy on the block, having practiced in U.S. tax issues for Canadians for many years. He is the author of *Brunton's U.S. Taxletter for Canadians*, and he has been our mentor for many years. He is a tremendous resource and a really wonderful man. We are grateful for his time and his encouragement of our writing efforts.

A dual citizen of Canada and the United States, Kevin Zemp of Bennett Jones in Calgary is a great friend and an excellent Canada-U.S. immigration attorney and resource. We have appreciated his support throughout this project.

Joe Kirkwood of Liebl and Kirkwood of Del Mar, California, is another outstanding U.S. immigration attorney who was kind enough to review the immigration section of this book. Joe and his partner Geoff, like Kevin, are dual citizens. Their firm is an outstanding resource for us and our clients, and we appreciate the opportunity to work with them.

Brian Wruk is not only my partner but truly a cherished friend. He has helped me to fulfill my dream of working with clients in both Canada and the United States. It was through his persistence and patience that this book and our other books became possible. I am grateful for all we have developed together.

Eva Sunderlin is simply the most incredible administrative colleague any two guys could have. Eva is our Canada-U.S. para-planner in our Arizona office and is the glue that keeps us all together. Unfortunately, given my hectic Canada-U.S. commuting schedule, I don't get to see her as often as I'd like. But I'm just grateful to know that she's a part of our lives.

I've had the occasion to work with some wonderful professionals over the years. They include Kim Moody, CA, a walking Canadian Income Tax Act, a great friend, and an incredible resource. Edward Northwood of the Ruchelman Law Firm (New York and Toronto) is one of the best Canada-U.S. tax and estate planning attorneys around, and I've been able to learn a tremendous amount from his expertise over the years. The same holds true for Mark Feigenbaum. I'd also like to acknowledge my former Royal Bank colleagues and friends, who include Jacinta McInnis, Prashant Patel, Geoff Anselmo, Len Rabey, and Lynda Dunfield, and finally Meghan Meger of bmo Harris in Calgary.

Thanks to our publisher, Jack David, of ECW Press, for believing in this book and the other books published on our behalf. Thanks also to our editor, Dallas Harrison, for the hours you've spent reviewing the manuscript and helping us to properly convey our message to our readers.

Sumita Chakrabarti of the Institute of Canadian Bankers, was a primary influence in putting the wheels in motion for this book. I appreciate your efforts on my behalf and your support.

Our clients, without whom our firms would not exist — we enjoy the variety of relationships with you and the opportunity to serve you. We appreciate your support for this project.

My family: my father, Michael S. Ritchie, of Ajijic, Mexico, and my mother, Catherine Ritchie, of Phoenix, Arizona — thank you for all you have done and continue to do for me. I appreciate your renewed love and support. My children, Jake, McKenna, Chase, and Evan — what a wonderful gift you are to me. Thanks for supporting me while I've been busy working on my book.

My beautiful and wonderful wife Margaret — I appreciate your love, patience, and unconditional support. I'm so grateful you are a part of my life.

And our readers — thank you for purchasing this book. We trust you will find it a useful reference as you either pursue or live your "snowbird" lifestyle in the United States. If you have any questions, comments, corrections, or things you'd like us to address in further editions, please e-mail us at snowbird@transitionfinancial.com. For further information on Canada-U.S. tax, estate, and financial planning matters, visit our website at www.transitionfinancial.com.

Terry F. Ritchie, cfp (U.S.), rfp, ea (U.S.), tep

Introduction

Every year hundreds of thousands of Canadians cross into the U.S. seeking warmer climates during those cold Canadian winters. These individuals are collectively referred to as "snowbirds." If you've purchased this book, it's likely because you, or someone you know, is a snowbird. Some of you may already be familiar with some of the unique financial, income, and estate tax issues that you face in the U.S., and this book will prove to be a valuable resource for you. For others, this book will provide you with the detailed information you need to help you navigate the slippery slope of becoming a snowbird.

According to the Royal Bank of Canada, over 1.5 million Canadians head south for the winter for a minimum of at least two months. The Canadian Snowbird Association suggests that more than 750,000 Canadian snowbirds head to the southern United States each winter for an average of 4.7 months. Regardless of which number it is or for how long, that's a lot of "birds flying south" for the winter.

While in the U.S., you will likely participate in financial transactions involving U.S. dollars. You might, for example, purchase a house or condominium in Arizona, Florida, California, Texas, or Hawaii. You might reside in it for a few months of the year, rent it out at other times, and hopefully sell it at a profit in the future — and in U.S. dollars! Some of you might get sick or suffer an accident while in the U.S. Unfortunately, some of you might pass away owning U.S. assets and have to pay the dreaded U.S. estate tax. It alone can compromise your retirement savings and in turn the future lifestyle of a surviving spouse. In addition, the confusion among family members that can arise in such circumstances can be mind-boggling and, in our experience, lead to hasty decisions with long-term effects.

Crossing the border, spending time in the U.S., and engaging in various financial transactions carry legal and tax implications both in Canada and in the U.S. The tax laws are distinctly different between the two countries. Becoming more aware of the financial, immigration, health care, tax planning, and estate planning issues that you will face allows you to make the most of your snowbird lifestyle.

Having practiced in the areas of Canada-U.S. financial and transition planning for many years and having written about the unique financial planning requirements of Canadians and Americans in both countries (see our companion books *The Canadian in America: Real Life Tax and Financial Insights into Moving and Living in the U.S.* and *The American in Canada: Real Life Tax and Financial Insights into Moving and Living in Canada*, both published by ECW Press), we thought a book specifically written for the needs of snowbirds was required.

It is not uncommon for us to work with snowbirds who ultimately decide to pursue their dream of permanent residence in the U.S. either through meeting and marrying a U.S. citizen or through potential U.S. immigration planning strategies. We hope this book is a good starting point for whatever type of lifestyle (temporary or permanent) you desire in the U.S. We have tried to cover the most common financial, immigration, tax, and estate planning issues that you will face as a snowbird.

In Chapter 1, "Don't Worry, I'll Be Back: Crossing the U.S. Border," we address

- the U.S. immigration requirements and implications of crossing the border,
- the documents you'll need when entering the U.S.,
- how to take money, personal items, and medication across the border, and
- additional tips to keep in mind when returning to Canada.

In Chapter 2, "Welcome to the U.S. — Now Pay Up! U.S. Tax Issues for Snowbirds," you will learn about

- your income tax filing requirements when in the U.S.,
- how the IRS determines your residency under U.S. tax rules,
- what the Substantial Presence Test is and why you should file IRS Form 8840 to avoid being taxed on your worldwide income,
- U.S. and Canadian tax treatment if you rent or sell your U.S. property,
- how to minimize and/or avoid having the IRS keep 10% of the sale proceeds of your U.S. real estate longer than necessary,
- the purposes of and requirements for obtaining a U.S. Individual Taxpayer Identification Number (ITIN),
- how to recover the tax withheld on your U.S. gambling winnings, and
- ways to avoid specific U.S. tax scams aimed at you.

In Chapter 3, "A Home Away from Home: Purchasing U.S. Real Estate," we help you to understand

- how to go about obtaining a mortgage for your U.S. property,
- the differences between U.S. and Canadian mortgages,

- new terms that you should be familiar with if you buy or mortgage U.S. property, and
- the ways in which you can title your U.S. real estate to minimize U.S. income and estate tax problems.

In Chapter 4, "Money Doesn't Grow on Trees: Money Management Issues for Snowbirds," we provide an overview of
- the Canadian banking packages available for snowbirds,
- what you need to know to open a bank account in the U.S.,
- how various forms of U.S. investment income are taxed in the U.S. and Canada,
- whether you can still manage your investment and retirement accounts in Canada while in the U.S.,
- effective strategies you can use to save money when exchanging Canadian loonies for U.S. dollars,
- how to calculate the exchange rate when you convert Canadian and U.S. dollars, and
- tips to help you manage and protect your credit and debit cards when in the U.S.

Chapter 5, "Till Death Do Us Part: U.S. Estate Planning Issues for Snowbirds," will help you to understand
- the dreaded U.S. estate tax and the assets subject to it,
- how critical the Canada-U.S. Income Tax Treaty is to your Canada-U.S. estate planning,
- what the future prospects of the U.S. estate tax might be and how it could affect you,
- how to calculate the U.S. estate tax,
- the most effective ways to reduce, defer, or eliminate U.S. estate tax,
- what the U.S. estate tax filing requirements to the IRS are for you and your executor, and
- the importance of making sure that your will and other legal documents properly address your temporary snowbird lifestyle.

In Chapter 6, "Help! I've Fallen, and I Can't Get Up: Risk Management Issues for Snowbirds," we deal with

- the implications of getting sick while in the U.S.,
- what your provincial health care plan will cover and what it won't,
- what you need to consider in selecting a travel insurance policy, and
- which additional features should be included on your property insurance policy while you are in the U.S.

In Chapter 7, "Mayday! Mayday! Finding Help," we provide you with an overview of

- how to select the right professional advisor to help you, and
- what to look for and the questions to ask before you hire him or her.

Finally, at the end of the book, we provide a number of relevant websites that you will find valuable. As well, we include a number of interesting Canada-U.S. tips that you will enjoy and can use to test your Canadian friends and your new American ones.

1

Don't Worry, I'll Be Back

Crossing the U.S. Border

Entering the United States

With the events of September 11, 2001, the ease with which Canadian snowbirds cross the American border changed dramatically. With the passing of the U.S. Western Hemisphere Travel Initiative (WHTI) in April 2005, significant changes are being implemented and still debated. At the time of writing and despite implementation of the WHTI, a number of Canadian politicians suggested that seniors should be exempt from having to obtain a passport, much like the exemption provided for children under the age of 15 in late February 2007. Regardless of what ultimately occurs, the U.S. Departments of State and Homeland Security are moving forward with implementation of WHTI along the timetable they have proposed. Earlier in 2007, the American ambassador to Canada, David Wilkins, in a speech on U.S.-Canada relations, responded to questions about the border-crossing changes by saying, "I believe we need to get ready for it, and so, simply put, the message I try to give to Americans and to Canadians is 'Get a passport.' It's that simple." In this case, we agree with Ambassador Wilkins' statement and advice because of the changes 9/11 brought to our countries. This chapter addresses issues you will face when crossing the American border and reviews the guidelines to obtain and maintain your Canadian passport.

The B-2 Visa

Despite the close relationship between Canada and the United States, anytime you cross the border you mustn't forget you are crossing into another country. When entering the United States, you can do so without the issuing of a U.S. immigration visa if your purpose is simply to spend your winters in the United States.

Under U.S. immigration rules, spending your winters in the United States is referred to as a temporary pleasure trip. The American visa category automatically assigned to you for this purpose is the B-2 visa. It is available to temporary visitors only and does not allow you to work or establish long-term residence in the United States. There is no application to complete, nor will you receive a visa document or stamp in your passport.

Under current rules, B-2 visitors are automatically entitled to be in the United States for a maximum of six months in the calendar year. Under this visa category, your stay in the United States must be temporary, and you must demonstrate a clear intention to depart prior to the end of the authorized period of your stay. If you leave the United States and reenter later, the six-month period starts over. However, you can't keep leaving the United States at the end of each six-month period and assume that a new six-month period has begun. Again, this must be distinguished from the "one-time" period granted by U.S. immigration once you make your entry at a U.S. border point. Repeated crossings back into the United States start to show intent to reside there, which means you are in violation of the visa issued to you and are now required to pay taxes, as outlined in Chapter 2.

Upon your entry into the United States, you must have the proper documentation to prove your origin and identity. Although a U.S. Customs and Border Protection (USCBP) officer may accept an oral declaration of your citizenship, it is recommended that at minimum you carry your passport and perhaps additional documents that establish citizenship or Canadian residency such as a birth certificate or driver's license. Under current USCBP procedures, all travelers are required to present photo identification. If you are not a Canadian citizen but a Canadian resident — such as a landed immigrant of Canada —different guidelines and procedures will be required when you cross into the United States. Copies of your non-immigrant visa in Canada and your passport from your country of birth are required.

You have to understand that it is a privilege to enter the United States, not an entitlement. Therefore, U.S. immigration can refuse entry to you if you have a previous criminal record or cannot show a legitimate reason why you are entering the United States. In terms of a past criminal conviction, it does not matter how long ago or how serious the offence was. If you have a previous criminal conviction, you should seek qualified American immigration counsel and complete U.S. Citizenship and Immigration Service (USCIS) Form I-192 — *Advance Permission to Enter as a Non-Immigrant.* Note that it could take a few months to process this form and could compromise your plans to visit the United States.

If you are traveling through an airport, you are required to complete USCBP Declaration Form 6059B, the blue card you typically fill out at the airport. This form requires personal information, including the purpose of your visit to the United States, information about where you are staying, what flight you are taking, as well as financial information related to the value of all goods you are bringing to leave in the United States.

Documents Required to Cross the U.S. Border

Ideally, the best documentation to have when entering the United States is a Canadian passport. In April 2005, the U.S. Departments of State and Homeland Security announced the Western Hemisphere Travel Initiative, which requires travelers from Canada, Mexico, and Bermuda entering the United States to carry a passport or other accepted document. Starting January 23, 2007, all Canadian citizens traveling by air from Canada are required to present a valid Canadian passport to enter or reenter the United States. This requirement includes citizens of the United States, Mexico, and Bermuda — and the children of citizens of those countries — as well. Those traveling by land and sea will need a passport by January 1, 2008. However, with the passing of the Homeland Security Appropriations Act on October 4, 2006, the U.S. Departments of State and Homeland Security now have until June 1, 2009, to implement the WHTI. Nevertheless, it is strongly recommended that you carry your Canadian passport when you leave and reenter Canada.

If you attempt to enter the United States without a valid Canadian passport, you will likely be referred to secondary screening at the airport or port of entry to the United States. If you've ever had the occasion to spend time in the secondary screening "lounge," you likely saw a number of anxious and concerned folks — the-deer-in-the-headlights look comes to mind — who wait "patiently" to be further evaluated by USCBP officers. These officers are not as concerned as you are about your flight or travel schedule and the like as they attempt to evaluate your evidence of citizenship and identification against their databases. It is for this reason that you should always carry a valid Canadian passport whenever you travel to the United States.

Obtaining a Canadian Passport

Canadian passports are valid for five years after the date of issue. They are not renewable. Therefore, it is important to keep track of the expiration date of your passport; you may be denied entry into the United States if your passport will expire during your time there. We recommend that, to avoid problems when entering the United States, you get a new passport before heading south for the winter.

The requirements to obtain a Canadian passport include

- completion of an adult passport application (Form PPTC 044),
- two identical photos taken within the past 12 months (no smiling),
- the application form and one of the photos signed by a guarantor, who can be a
  o chiropractor
  o dentist
  o geoscientist
  o judge
  o lawyer (member of a provincial bar association), notary in Quebec
  o magistrate
  o mayor
  o medical doctor
  o minister of religion authorized under provincial law to perform marriages
  o notary public
  o optometrist
  o pharmacist
  o police officer (municipal, provincial, or RCMP)
  o postmaster
  o principal of a primary or secondary school
  o professional accountant (APA, CA, CGA, CMA, PA, RPA)
  o professional engineer (P.Eng., Eng. in Quebec)
  o senior administrator in a community college (includes CEGEPS)
  o senior administrator or teacher in a university
  o veterinarian,
- proof of Canadian citizenship,
- proof of any previous Canadian travel document issued

within the past five years, and

- any document that supports your identity, such as a driver's license, social insurance card, or provincial health card.

The passport processing fee is $87 for a 24-page passport and $92 for a 48-page passport. We think this is the best deal you are going to get from the government: five more loonies for an extra 24 pages! Additional information on applying for a Canadian passport can be found at www.ppt.gc.ca or by calling 1-800-567-6868.

The Border Binder

If you make frequent trips to the United States, its immigration officials may question you about your residency intentions. To avoid this questioning, carry documented evidence to prove that your intention is not to establish permanent American residence. To that end, we recommend you carry a "border binder" with you to support your Canadian residency position. Let us explain the basis of this binder.

My family and I moved from Canada to the United States in 1979. My father, my siblings, and I were all issued green cards through the sponsorship of my mother, who is a U.S. citizen. I held my green card for 15 years and never expected that I would return to Canada. Although I could have and likely should have applied for American citizenship, I never got around to doing it. For unexpected personal reasons in 1995, my wife, my children, and I returned to Canada. When I returned to Canada with a U.S. green card, I was ultimately deemed to have abandoned my green card a few years later. From U.S. immigration's perspective, I had given up what to some was "the greatest gift in the world." As a result, every time I reentered the United States to visit family and friends, to attend or speak at a professional conference, or to develop business, I was given a harder time than others and was sometimes referred to secondary processing for further questioning. Given my past ties to the United States, the frequency of my visits and the fact that I had family and business dealings there, the officials wanted to make sure I was not trying to reestablish U.S. permanent residency again.

As a means of proving my Canadian residency ties and ultimately to "speed up" my American border processing, I decided to purchase a small three-ring binder and several clear plastic inserts. I then assembled all relevant original documents that confirmed my Canadian residency position and put them in the plastic pages. My own border binder contained my birth certificate, passport, most recently filed Canadian tax returns, land title certificate, annual property assessment from the City of Calgary, copy of my driver's license, and recent utility bills (gas, electricity, phone, etc.). The first time I took my binder with me, the officer was quite impressed about how well organized I was and put me right through. I continued to take my binder with me just in case I was ever scrutinized. Fortunately, with my border binder in hand, I did not have any further problems crossing the border.

To ease your border crossing each winter, you should consider creating your own border binder and include the following documents:

- a photocopy of your land title certificate to verify ownership of your Canadian principal residence or, if you rent, a copy of your rental agreement;
- recent utility bills (telephone, cable, power, gas);
- your property tax bill or annual assessment from the city or municipality;
- a valid provincial driver's license confirming your residential address;
- your vehicle registration if driving and return flight tickets if flying;
- a provincial health care card and/or copy of your travel insurance policy or certificate;
- copies of your most recently filed Canadian tax return and

notice of assessment; and

- a previously filed IRS Form 8840 (see Chapter 2 for further information).

Automated Entry/Exit System?

In 1996, the U.S. Congress mandated an entry/exit system (as part of the Illegal Immigration Reform and Immigrant Responsibility Act or IIRAIRA — the Americans love their acronyms!), but due to objections from the tourism industry, governors of many states bordering Canada, and others, full implementation of this system has been delayed. Over the past number of years, and particularly in light of the tragic events of 9/11, there has been ongoing debate about the implementation and effectiveness of an automated entry/exit system at Canadian-U.S. border crossings.

Attending a conference a few years ago, I questioned an official with one of the American consulates in Canada about the likelihood of such a system at the Canadian-U.S. border crossings. He suggested that it was only a matter of time before such a system would be implemented. Although there isn't a system in place specifically to track Canadian citizens into the United States, the country now has the U.S. VISIT (U.S. Visitor and Immigrant Status Indication Technology) system in place at many airports and seaports. This is an electronic check-in/check-out system for foreign visitors, including students, tourists, and business travelers, and requires the use of at least two biometric identifiers, such as fingerprints, when entering and leaving the United States.

At the time of writing, Canadian citizens were still exempt from this system. Interestingly enough, a COMPASS-*National Post*-Global National poll conducted in April 2003 found that Canadians themselves do not object to being included in a U.S. entry/exit system, while more than 70% indicated that the United States has the right to track the entry and exit of all foreign visitors, including Canadians.

Outside the practical reasons for having such a system, the

information obtained by uscis can be used to further assist agencies in both Canada and the United States to ensure you are complying with U.S. income tax, immigration, and provincial health care rules. That is, such a system would track the number of days you are in the United States to ensure you are not staying there for longer than six months. The intent is also to ensure your compliance with irs Form 8840 (see Chapter 2 for further information).

U.S. Retirement Visa?

Many countries around the world offer "retirement visas" that allow you to retire and live permanently in those countries. For example, my father, a dual citizen (Canada/United States), has lived in Mexico for the past 10 years on such a visa. To the extent that one can prove financial solvency and cover health care risks, retirement visas from certain countries are available. Many snowbirds have wondered if such a visa will ever be available in the United States.

A number of years ago, a former Florida Republican congressman, Bill McCollum, attempted to lobby support for such a visa. However, he was defeated in 2000 and further as a Senate candidate in 2004. As a result, the efforts toward such a visa have likely gone by the wayside for the foreseeable future. In fact, with other priorities occupying the American government at this time — Iraq, the war on global terrorism, curbing the tide of illegal immigration — we believe such a visa likely will never see the light of day. Of course, we were wrong, along with others, that the Canadian dollar would ever break through the U.S.80¢ level during our lifetimes.

Crossing the Border with More than $10,000
Canadian Rules

When crossing the border into the United States, you may be required to show that you have enough money to adequately provide for yourself while there. There are no restrictions on the amount of money you can take out of or bring into Canada (it is your money after all!). However, how you take your money out of and into Canada becomes the concern of the governments involved. We recommend you don't take any significant amounts of cash (greater than c$10,000), traveler's checks, money orders, stock or bond certificates, or other negotiable instruments with you.

For amounts in excess of c$10,000, or its equivalent in U.S. dollars, you must declare that amount at the Canadian border when you leave, and it just stands to reason that you will be detained and asked to explain its source and why you are carrying that much money with you. You will also be asked to complete Form E677 — *Cross-Border Currency or Monetary Instruments Report* — Individual and file it with the Canada Border Services Agency (CBSA).

If you are sending c$10,000 or more — or its equivalent in U.S. dollars — to the United States by regular or express mail, you are required to complete Form E667 and mail or submit it to the nearest Canada Customs office at the same time (or before) you mail it to the United States.

If you are sending in excess of c$10,000 — or its equivalent in U.S. dollars — through another individual or by courier, that individual/courier is required to complete Form E668 — *Cross-Border Currency or Monetary Instruments Report Made by Person in Charge of Conveyance* and attach it to Form E667. These forms should be filed with the Canada Border Services Agency as well.

American Rules

From an American perspective, if the amount is greater than U.S.$10,000, you need to fill out U.S. Department of Treasury Financial Crimes Enforcement Network Form 105 — *Report of International Transportation of Currency or Monetary Instruments* and file it with U.S. Customs and Border Protection.

As in Canada, this form applies to anyone who physically

enters the United States or mails in excess of U.S.$10,000 in currency or equivalent financial instruments to the United States. This form must also be filed by any individual in the United States who receives greater than U.S.$10,000 in currency or financial instruments.

If you fail to file the required Canadian or American forms, sizable monetary penalties, including confiscation of the money or financial instrument, could occur. Given that "big brother" is truly upon us, the information on these forms is sent to the Financial Transactions and Reports Analysis Centre (FINTRAC) in Ottawa for its review and assessment. For American purposes, the form is part of the Department of Treasury Financial Crimes Enforcement Network (FINCEN). The purpose of FINTRAC and FINCEN is to help stem the threat of money laundering and terrorist activity financing in both Canada and the United States.

To avoid hassle and administrative complications, we recommend that transfers of large amounts of money to and from Canada be sent electronically through preestablished channels, such as a wire from a bank. These are traceable transactions, and it is the financial institution's requirement to fill out the myriad forms on your behalf and ensure they are filed with the appropriate authorities. Note that your Canadian financial institution automatically reports any cash transactions (deposits or transfers) in excess of C$10,000 on Form E667 — *Cross-Border Currency or Monetary Instruments Report — General* to the Canada Border Services Agency. Transactions in excess of U.S.$10,000 are automatically reported by the American financial institution on FINCEN Form 104 — *Currency Transaction Report and Filed with U.S. Customs and Border Protection.*

Taking Medication to the States

Taking medication to the United States can present an interesting conundrum. Numerous issues arise when, for example, medications approved in Canada as "over the counter" (medications with codeine) require a prescription in the United States or when certain medications that have received approval to be offered to the American public (Aleve) are not approved in Canada. If you are planning to take medications to the United States, take only enough for your personal use for the time you will be away. If you plan on taking a little more as a preventative measure, be prepared to support your position, for a U.S. border official might question how long you are planning to stay in the United States. Make sure your medications are clearly labeled, in your name, and in the original containers with original labels to prevent anyone from mistaking them for other substances. You might consider carrying a copy of your original prescription to confirm that the medication is required or in case it is lost or stolen. Also consider carrying a list of phone numbers of your physician and pharmacist in case of emergency while in the United States. Some over-the-counter drugs that do not require a prescription in Canada — such as drugs that contain codeine — are not allowed into the United States without a prescription, so you may want to ask your physician to give you a letter stating the medical reason for the medication and the recommended dosage.

In Canada, common allergy and cold medicines containing pseudoephedrine or ephedrine can generally be readily purchased off the shelf in unlimited quantities. However, with the ever-growing methamphetamine problem in the United States, many states have instituted new procedures to curb the manufacture of this very dangerous and addictive drug. In Arizona, for example, only the label is on display in most drugstores. You have to take a card with the quantity and brand you want up to the prescription counter at the back of the store. An attendant will then ask you for your driver's license, and you will then provide your name, address, and phone number and sign a logbook. These logbooks are collected by local drug enforcement officials and consolidated into a database to see if any patterns of high purchases develop. The system is far from foolproof but is indicative of how these types of drugs will be dispensed in the future, so be wary of taking them with you to the United States, and consider purchasing them when you are down there.

If you are planning on flying to the United States, you should carry your medications with you instead of packing them in your checked luggage so you'll have ready access to them in case your luggage is lost or stolen. If you are planning on driving to the United States, avoid extreme temperatures. Do not store your prescriptions in your glove compartment or trunk, where temperatures can become extreme either way. Also don't leave your medications on the dashboard of your car or RV, where they are visible or can be exposed to direct sunlight.

If you are fortunate enough to have any young family members or friends visit you down south, make sure that your medications are out of their reach and stored away with child-resistant lids. Also make sure that the child's parent or guardian is aware of where your medications are stored.

Taking Pets to the States

As you head south for the winter, it is tough to leave some of your "other" family members at home. However, before you load up "Fluffy," "Fido," or "Schnooky" and head for the border, you should be aware there are certain requirements when taking pets to the United States. First, you will need a health certificate from your pet's veterinarian proving your pet has a clean bill of health. Second, each pet will also need a letter from its veterinarian confirming it is coming from a rabies-free zone. In lieu of this letter, you must show proof that your pets (dogs) have had valid rabies shots at least 30 days prior to entering the United States. Depending on which border crossing you use when you enter the United States, your pets will have to go through a pre-clearance process at that entry point by U.S. Customs. Note that any unusual or exotic pets (including Canadian beavers) might be barred from entry into the United States. You should call U.S. Customs in advance of your trip to determine if there are any additional requirements.

Taking Personal Items to the States

For some of you, going without your favorite hairbrush, good Canadian cheese, or favorite beer when wintering in the United States is unthinkable. There are some things you need to consider when heading for warmer weather. The following items can be taken across the border on a duty-free basis:

- 200 cigarettes, 50 cigars, or two kilograms of tobacco per person (note that Cuban cigars are generally prohibited in the United States even for personal use);
- up to one liter of alcoholic beverages for personal use per person;
- gifts up to U.S.$100 per person; and
- personal and household effects for individual use.

You must declare any food products, specifically meat, fruit, vegetables, and plants. In many cases, such items are confiscated — like our jumbo Costco Granny Smith apple that was taken by a U.S. Customs official in Sweet Grass, Montana, just before lunch (we should have eaten it on the way to the border!).

Driving Your Vehicle to the States

In the majority of cases, snowbirds tend to drive their own vehicles to the United States so they have a convenient means of getting around when down there. If you plan to do likewise, it is important to keep the following in mind.

- Make sure that your vehicle registration and driver's license are current and will not expire while you are away.
- Make sure that your automobile insurance will cover you for any claims that might occur while you are in the United States.
- Consider the role of roadside assistance. With a long drive ahead of you, it could be costly and dangerous to break down in what could be very unfamiliar surroundings or weather

conditions. Consider alternatives such as the Canadian Automobile Association or your auto manufacturer's programs that may provide assistance such as towing, tire changing, fuel replacement, travel books, and maps.

• If you are going to cross into Mexico, leave your vehicle in the United States or be sure you have the necessary auto insurance (and pay a bit extra for the legal representation in case you need it).

If you are contemplating flying down and having your vehicle shipped or driven down for you, you need to complete U.S. Customs Form 3299 — *Declaration for Free Entry of Unaccompanied Articles.* Along with this document, copies of your passport and vehicle registration are required. It's better not to have personal items in the vehicle when it is being shipped or driven down. These items could lead to potential challenges by American or Canadian Customs officials.

The Use of Canadian Satellite TV in the States

Being away from Canada means being away from Canadian television. This means you may have to miss the *Tim Hortons Brier*, *Hockey Night in Canada*, *The Royal Canadian Air Farce*, *Little Mosque on the Prairie*, and *Corner Gas* during the months you are away. Because these shows are next to impossible to find on American television (you can find *The Red Green Show* pretty easily), some snowbirds choose to take their Canadian satellite receivers down to the United States and plug them into their already installed satellite dishes.

In Canada, there are two primary satellite providers: Bell ExpressVu (www.bell.ca, 1-888-759-3474) and Star Choice (www.starchoice.com, 1-866-782-7932). Both services provide a broad lineup of television channels, including local Canadian television stations, American programming, and specialty channels. However, when it comes to the legality of taking your

Canadian satellite receiver to the United States, the two providers have different policies. According to the folks at Bell ExpressVu, their policy is that it is illegal to receive programming with their system while you are in the United States. However, the policy at Star Choice is that, as long as you have an account in Canada with a Canadian residential address, it has no problem with you taking your receiver and using its satellite system in the United States.

Another legal alternative that I use to watch Canadian television programming while in the United States is to purchase a Slingbox (www.slingmedia.com). A Slingbox is a small unit that sits on top of your television, satellite receiver, cable receiver, or digital video receiver (DVR) in Canada and allows you to watch Canadian television through your personal computer (laptop or desktop) while in the United States. In fact, you control your television back in Canada through your computer while in the United States. It's all done through the Internet and your computer, and it's very simple to set up and use. I read about this device a little over a year ago in the *Wall Street Journal* and finally decided to try it. I use it in my Arizona home and office when away from Canada. You can schedule the taping of programs through your DVR and wake up and watch your local Canadian morning news show on your computer to check out the wonderful weather conditions back home. This gives us the necessary fodder for all those e-mails we craftily design for family and friends back home. These devices cost between $170 and $280 (depending on the box you choose) and can be purchased at Future Shop, Best Buy, and London Drugs in Canada. You give up a bit on your viewing experience because it has to be done in front of your computer instead of your big-screen TV, but it still keeps you up to date. There are devices available to plug a computer into your big screen, so you may not have to suffer much at all.

Coming Back Home

When returning to Canada, you should maintain a list of all the items you purchased or acquired in the United States accompanying you back to Canada. Keeping receipts whenever possible is an excellent way to prove the value of the items and the length of time you've been out of the country for CBSA purposes. You should note that all items purchased in the United States must be declared. If you have been gone for more than seven days, you are allowed to bring back items valued up to C$750 tax and duty free. With the exception of tobacco products and alcoholic beverages, you do not need to have the goods with you when you arrive. You must personally declare tobacco and alcohol, which have the following limits:

- 200 cigarettes, 50 cigars, 200 grams (7 ounces) of tobacco, and 200 tobacco sticks;
- alcohol for personal use to a maximum of 1.14 liters (40 ounces) of liquor, 1.5 liters (53 imperial ounces) of wine, or 24 cans or bottles (355 milliliters each or 8.5 liters) of beer.

If you are considering taking an expensive item such as your television, VCR/DVD player, or camera into the United States, you should have a receipt or some other verification of purchase to confirm that the item was purchased in Canada. This is required not upon entry into the United States but as proof upon return to Canada that the items were indeed acquired in Canada.

Additional Tips

- Make sure your passport and/or driver's license will not expire when you are away.
- Make sure you have enough prescription medication to last while you are away from Canada.
- If traveling by car, let your friends and family know the route you are taking, and stay in contact with them until your final destination.

- Take a cell phone (make sure your coverage area includes the United States) *and* charger.
- Make sure your car is stocked with emergency provisions.
- Track your days to make sure you do not compromise your U.S. immigration and tax status (see Chapter 2 for more details).

2

Welcome to the United States —Now Pay Up!

U.S. Tax Issues for Snowbirds

U.S. Income Tax Filing Requirements of Snowbirds

So you think by leaving Canada for a few cold months you can escape the wrath of the Canada Revenue Agency (CRA)? Well, think again. Not only will the CRA still be waiting for you upon your return, but also its close friend, the American IRS, and certain state taxing agencies will be welcoming you with open arms. Spending time in the United States, buying or renting U.S. real estate, or celebrating your U.S. gambling winnings will likely create a much closer relationship with the CRA and the IRS than you might like.

The U.S. taxes individuals based on citizenship and residency, while Canada generally taxes individuals based on residency, *not* citizenship. Citizens of the United States and lawful permanent residents ("green card" holders) are taxed on their worldwide income, no matter where they live in the world

19

(see our companion book *The American in Canada*). Under American rules, individuals who are not U.S. citizens are referred to as "aliens." How a snowbird is taxed in the United States is determined by your status as either a *resident alien* or a *non-resident alien*.

This is an important distinction. A resident alien is taxed on worldwide income in much the same manner as an American citizen. Such individuals are required to file U.S. income tax returns and pay U.S. tax on their worldwide income (from all sources, from all locations). When computing taxable income, a resident alien is generally entitled to the same deductions and personal exemptions available to an American citizen. Non-resident aliens, on the other hand, are generally taxed on their income from U.S. sources only, with some exceptions. Deductions and exemptions available to non-resident aliens are limited.

A snowbird will be treated as a resident for tax purposes if he or she meets either of two tests: the lawful permanent resident (or green card) test, or the substantial presence test.

The Green Card Test

Under this test, a Canadian citizen who is a lawful permanent resident of the United States — a green card holder — is considered a resident for U.S. income tax purposes. A green card holder is treated as an American resident whether or not the individual is physically present in the United States, until such time as permanent resident alien status under American immigration law is officially revoked or abandoned. This means that, if you are an American green card holder living in Canada most of the time but snowbirding in the United States, you must file U.S. income tax returns every year and declare and be taxed on your worldwide income.

For further information related to the taxation of Canadians who are also green card holders or American citizens who live in Canada, see our companion books *The Canadian in America* and *The American in Canada*.

The Substantial Presence Test

Under the second test, a snowbird may become an American resident for tax purposes if he or she spends a substantial portion of time in the United States. The substantial presence test is a formula under U.S. tax law that calculates the number of days that an individual spends in the United States over a three-year period; if the limit is exceeded, the person becomes an American resident for tax purposes (but not for immigration purposes).

To determine whether you meet this test for the "current year," add up the

1. number of days present in the United States in the current year, plus
2. one-third of the days present in the United States in the preceding year, plus
3. one-sixth of the days present in the United States in the second preceding year.

If this total equals *183 days or more*, and you spend more than 31 days in the United States in the current year, you are considered a resident alien for the current year. If this total equals *182 days or less*, you are considered a non-resident alien for the current year. Consider the following examples.

Example 1: Non-Resident Alien

Year	Days Present in United States	Equivalent Days
Current Year	120	120
t-1	120 x 1/3	40
t-2	120 x 1/6	20
Total		180

Because the days calculated in this example are fewer than 183, you are not considered a resident of the United States for income tax purposes.

Example 2: Resident Alien

Year	Days Present in United States	Equivalent Days
Current Year	130	130
t-1	120 x 1/3	40
t-2	120 x 1/6	20
Total		190

Because the days calculated in this example are greater than 183, you are considered a resident of the United States for income tax purposes.

Therefore, if you consistently spend your winters in the United States, be aware of the requirements the substantial presence test places on you and whether you are considered an American resident for income tax purposes. If this is the case, you are required to file a U.S. 1040 income tax return and report your worldwide income (including all your income from Canada) on this return.

As a general rule, if you do not spend more than 121 days (approximately four months) in the United States in any tax year, you will never be considered an American resident under the substantial presence test. What is interesting about this is you don't need any form of working immigration status to become a tax resident for U.S. purposes! This creates an interesting conundrum: a B-1 or B-2 visitor's visa allows you to remain in the United States for up to six months, but neither allows you to earn wages there. However, you are substantially present in the United States (and considered a tax resident for U.S. purposes) if you have been there for 183 days or more in one year over the past three years and have to file a U.S. 1040 tax return.

If you spent any days in the United States because you were unable to leave due to a medical condition that arose while there, those days will not count. U.S. tax laws treat presence in the United States for a medical condition as non-U.S. days.

It is important to note that, even though you could be deemed a resident for U.S. income tax purposes, this does not give you the right to actually live or work in the United States. That right is only granted under separate American immigration laws as discussed in Chapter 1.

If you meet the substantial presence test, all is not lost, though. Two exceptions allow you to be considered a non-resident of the United States. These exceptions are referred to as *the closer connection exception and the tax treaty tie-breaker provisions.*

The Closer Connection Exception

If you meet the substantial presence test but maintain a closer connection to Canada, you won't meet the test for the current year if

- you are present in the United States fewer than 183 days during the current year, and
- you maintain a tax home (your main place of business or employment; or, if you have no such place, the place where you regularly live) in Canada during the current year, and
- you have a closer connection during the current year to a single foreign country — Canada — in which you maintain a tax home greater than that in the United States.

You can generally establish that your tax home is in Canada by showing that your principal place of business/employment and/or home is located in Canada. The tax home must be in existence for the entire taxable year and must be in the foreign country to which you claim a closer connection. Thus, the closer connection exception generally doesn't apply in the year you physically move to the United States since your principal dwelling place is no longer located in Canada (see our companion book *The Canadian in America* for further information).

The IRS determines your closer connection to Canada by weighing your connections to the United States compared with those to Canada. Such connections include the location of your

- regular or principal permanent home,
- family,
- automobiles,
- personal belongings,
- banks where you conduct your routine personal banking,
- registration to vote, and
- investments.

In previous years, the IRS also required information related to any social, cultural, religious, and political organizations in which you participated as well as any charitable organizations to which you contributed. However, effective after tax year 2006, this information is no longer required.

To claim the closer connection exception, you must file IRS Form 8840 — *Closer Connection Exception Statement for Aliens* (reproduced below) on or before June 15th of the year following the year you met the substantial presence test. If Form 8840 is not filed in a timely manner, the right to claim the exception for that tax year might be lost, and you could be deemed a resident of the United States and would be required to file a 1040 tax return and declare your worldwide income.

The purpose of this form is to advise the IRS that your tax home is indeed in Canada and that you maintained more significant ties in Canada than in the United States during the current year. Each person claiming the closer connection exception has to file Form 8840. Therefore, if you are married and/or have children with you in the United States who also meet the substantial presence test, each person is required to file Form 8840 to claim the closer connection exception.

If you have been snowbirding in the United States for the past few years, you are likely aware of the filing requirements of Form 8840 and, as the upstanding and honorable Canadian you are, have been annually filing this form on a timely basis. However, in our experience, many Canadians meet the substantial presence test but don't file the form as you do. Often the flippant answer we get is "What can the IRS do?" You've likely never heard or read about any bad publicity about those who are not filing Form 8840. Let us get up on our soapbox for a moment. First, as we discussed earlier, "big brother" is becoming more of a threat each passing day, and the ability of the IRS and the U.S. Citizenship and Immigration Service (USCIS) to share information and to track your days in the United States for income tax, immigration, or provincial health care administration will soon be a computer keystroke away. Second, those who don't remain in compliance with the laws of the land still regard their entry into the United States as a right, not a privilege. If you want to enjoy the warm weather in the United States and take advantage of what the country has to offer you as a visitor, you should comply with the laws of the land.

Besides, filing this form is relatively simple and will give you greater peace of mind when you are in the United States. Conceivably, if you don't file Form 8840, you could be deemed an American resident for income tax purposes and then meet a whole other set of U.S. tax filing and compliance problems. Not only could the IRS tax you on your worldwide income, but also you would be required to file U.S. Department of Treasury Form TD F 90-22.12 — *Report on Foreign Bank and Financial Accounts*, requiring you to disclose your financial accounts in Canada — including RRSPs or RIFFs. Failure to do so could lead to criminal prosecution, with penalties as high as U.S.$500,000 and 10 years in jail! That would likely solve your Form 8840 annual filing requirements for a while! In addition, you may be subject to significant penalties for not filing IRS Form 3520 to report your interest in Canadian mutual funds, income trusts, and registered

Form **8840**

Department of the Treasury
Internal Revenue Service

Closer Connection Exception Statement for Aliens

▶ Attach to Form 1040NR or Form 1040NR-EZ.

For the year January 1—December 31, 2006, or other tax year
beginning _____ , 2006, and ending _____ , 20____ .

OMB No. 1545-0074

2006

Attachment
Sequence No. **101**

Your first name and initial	Last name	Your U.S. taxpayer identification number, if any

Fill in your addresses only if you are filing this form by itself and not with your U.S. tax return

Address in country of residence	Address in the United States

Part I   General Information

1 Type of U.S. visa (for example, F, J, M, etc.) and date you entered the United States ▶ _____

2 Of what country or countries were you a citizen during the tax year? _____

3 What country or countries issued you a passport? _____

4 Enter your passport number(s) ▶ _____

5 Enter the number of days you were present in the United States during:
2006 _____   2005 _____   2004 _____ .

6 During 2006, did you apply for, or take other affirmative steps to apply for, lawful permanent resident status in the United States or have an application pending to change your status to that of a lawful permanent resident of the United States (see instructions)? . . . . ☐ **Yes** ☐ **No**

Part II   Closer Connection to One Foreign Country

7 Where was your tax home during 2006? _____

8 Enter the name of the foreign country to which you had a closer connection than to the United States during 2006
▶ _____

Next, complete Part IV on the back.

Part III   Closer Connection to Two Foreign Countries

9 Where was your tax home on January 1, 2006? _____

10 After changing your tax home from its location on January 1, 2006, where was your tax home for the remainder of 2006? _____

11 Did you have a closer connection to each foreign country listed on lines 9 and 10 than to the United States for the period during which you maintained a tax home in that foreign country? . . . . . ☐ **Yes** ☐ **No**
If "No," attach an explanation.

12 Were you subject to tax as a resident under the internal laws of **(a)** either of the countries listed on lines 9 and 10 during all of 2006 or **(b)** both of the countries listed on lines 9 and 10 for the period during which you maintained a tax home in each country? . . . . ☐ **Yes** ☐ **No**

13 Have you filed or will you file tax returns for 2006 in the countries listed on lines 9 and 10? . . . ☐ **Yes** ☐ **No**
If "Yes" to either line 12 or line 13, attach verification.
If "No" to either line 12 or line 13, please explain ▶ _____

Next, complete Part IV on the back.

For Paperwork Reduction Act Notice, see page 4.   Cat. No. 15829P   Form **8840** (2006)

Part IV   **Significant Contacts With Foreign Country or Countries in 2006**

14   Where was your regular or principal permanent home located during 2006 (see instructions)? ....

15   If you had more than one permanent home available to you at all times during 2006, list the location of each and explain ▶ ....

16   Where was your family located?   ....

17   Where was your automobile(s) located?   ....

18   Where was your automobile(s) registered? ....
      ....

19   Where were your personal belongings, furniture, etc., located?   ....
      ....

20   Where was the bank(s) with which you conducted your routine personal banking activities located?

 a   _____   c   _____

 b   _____   d   _____

21   Did you conduct business activities in a location other than your tax home? . . . . ☐ **Yes**   ☐ **No**
      If "Yes," where?   ....

22a Where was your driver's license issued? ....

 b   If you hold a second driver's license, where was it issued?   ....
      ....

23   Where were you registered to vote?   ....

24   When completing official documents, forms, etc., what country do you list as your residence? ....

25   Have you ever completed:

 a   Form W-8 or Form W-8BEN (relating to foreign status)?   . . . . ☐ **Yes**   ☐ **No**

 b   Form W-9, Request for Taxpayer Identification Number and Certification?   . . . . ☐ **Yes**   ☐ **No**

 c   Form 1078, Certificate of Alien Claiming Residence in the United States?   . . . . ☐ **Yes**   ☐ **No**

 d   Any other U.S. official forms? If "Yes," indicate the form(s) ▶   .... ☐ **Yes**   ☐ **No**

26   In what country/countries did you keep your personal, financial, and legal documents? ....
      ....

27   From what country/countries did you derive the majority of your 2006 income? ....
      ....

28   Did you have any income from U.S. sources? . . . . ☐ **Yes**   ☐ **No**
      If "Yes," what type?   ....

29   In what country/countries were your investments located (see instructions)? ....
      ....

30   Did you qualify for any type of government-sponsored "national" health plan? . . . . ☐ **Yes**   ☐ **No**
      If "Yes," in what country?   ....
      If "No," please explain ▶   ....
      If you have any other information to substantiate your closer connection to a country other than the United States or you wish to explain in more detail any of your responses to lines 14 through 30, attach a statement to this form.

Sign here only if you are filing this form by itself and not with your U.S. tax return	Under penalties of perjury, I declare that I have examined this form and the accompanying attachments, and to the best of my knowledge and belief, they are true, correct, and complete.
	▶ _____ ▶ _____
	Your signature Date

assets. In this case, the penalties could be as high as 5% of the value of your investments and up to 35% of any distributions from your Canadian investments, trusts, and registered plans! Finally, if you have an interest in a Canadian company, another myriad of IRS filing requirements and penalties could be imposed, such as filing Form 5471. So, bottom line, if you meet the substantial presence test, file Form 8840 and sleep easier while you are in the United States. The risks of not filing Form 8840 are becoming greater every day.

Canada-U.S. Tax Treaty Tie-Breaker Provisions

It is possible that you could be considered a resident of both Canada and the United States pursuant to the tax laws in each country. The Canada-U.S. Income Tax Convention (the "treaty") then comes into play so you won't be considered a resident of both countries. These key tie-breaker rules are as follows.

1. An individual shall be deemed a resident solely of the country in which he or she has a permanent home available.
2. If a permanent home is available in both countries, or if a permanent home is not available in either country, the individual will be deemed to be a resident solely in the country with which his or her personal and economic relations are closer (center of vital interests).
3. If the center of vital interests cannot be determined, he or she will be deemed to be a resident of the country in which he or she has a habitual abode.
4. If a habitual abode is available in both countries or in neither country, he or she will be deemed to be a resident of the country of which he or she is a citizen.
5. If he or she is a citizen of both countries, or of neither, the competent authorities of the countries will settle the question by mutual agreement.

In our practice, we have seen situations in which a snowbird clearly meets the substantial presence test *and* spends more than

183 days in the United States in the current year. In this case, not only have these individuals broken U.S. immigration laws (the B-2 visa is issued for only six months), but also they are no longer eligible to file Form 8840. In this case, such individuals are required to file IRS Form 1040NR — *U.S. Nonresident Alien Income Tax Return* and Form 8833 — *Treaty-Based Return Position Disclosure under Section 6114 or 7701(b)* to claim relief under the Canada-U.S. Tax Treaty. This tax return must be filed in a timely manner to claim the treaty tie-breaker provisions. Failure to file this return may result in significant penalties.

The risk of taking this filing position is that you could compromise your future U.S. immigration status. If U.S. immigration officials question you about your extra days in the United States or find out through alternative means, you risk losing the ability to snowbird in the United States in the future. You could also be at risk with your provincial health care plan because you are out of the province for more than six months (see Chapter 6). Now you can see why the government is working on an automated entry/exit system to assist immigration, tax, and provincial health care agencies.

If you hold an American green card, further complications arise. In this situation, a snowbird who holds a green card but is a resident of Canada claiming to be a non-resident of the United States per the treaty could cause the green card to be forfeited. The U.S. Income Tax Regulations (Internal Revenue Code) provide that claiming non-resident status may affect the determination by USCIS as to whether you qualify to maintain your green card or not. We recommend you consult with a competent Canada-U.S. immigration attorney before taking any action.

Taxation of the Rental of U.S. Real Estate

Many snowbirds own a home or condominium vacation property in the United States. In some cases, you may choose to rent out the property to friends, family, or others while you are not using it. If this is the case, you should be aware of the American and Canadian tax implications of renting your U.S. property.

U.S. Tax Implications

Under American tax rules, the IRS allows you to have your U.S.-source rental income taxed in one of two ways:

(1) through the remittance of withholding tax on gross rents, or
(2) through the filing of Form 1040NR, a non-resident income tax return.

Generally, if you remit a 30% withholding tax on the gross rents received from the property, your tax obligation has been fulfilled with the IRS. Gross rents refer to all rents received without any deductions for ordinary expenses against the property.

The way to lower your taxes on your rental income is by filing a U.S. income tax return on a net rental income basis. This is your gross rents less any ordinary expenses (property taxes, mortgage interest, insurance, management fees, utilities, etc.). Also note that a deduction for depreciation (capital cost allowance for Canadian tax purposes) is mandatory for U.S. income tax filing purposes.

Generally, most snowbirds who rent out their American real estate property are better off filing a tax return on a net basis. The net rental income amount subject to U.S. tax at the marginal tax rate will likely be substantially lower than the amount subject to the 30% withholding tax.

Filing Form 1040NR must be done in a timely manner in order for you to file on a net basis. You should file this form along with Schedule E by June 15th of the year following the year in which you received rental income. If this deadline is missed, there is an additional 16 months of grace before you can no longer take your deductions. At that point, the 30% withholding tax on gross rental income, along with the applicable penalties and interest, would apply.

Depending on the state in which your property is located, a state income tax return may be required as well. Below are listed the tax forms to be filed for some of the most common snowbird states.

- Florida — no state income tax filing requirement
- Texas — no state income tax filing requirement
- Arizona — Form 140NR
- California — Form 540NR
- Hawaii — Form N-15

If the property does not generate net rental income (gross income less expenses and mandatory depreciation), a state income tax return doesn't need to be filed.

Canadian Tax Implications

Since you are still a Canadian tax resident and required to declare your worldwide income, any net rental income, adjusted for Canadian dollars, must also be reported on your Canadian tax return Form T776. To eliminate any double taxation, you should take any tax paid in the United States as a foreign tax credit on your Canadian return. This is a tricky undertaking, and we recommend you seek competent Canada-U.S. tax preparation help to ensure you eliminate any double taxation.

Example of the Tax Implications of Renting a U.S. Property

Let's assume you purchased a vacation property in Sarasota, Florida, several years ago. You recently experienced some health problems that limit your time there, so you want to determine the tax implications if you rent out your Florida property during the winter months. The property is now worth U.S.$250,000 and is owned jointly with your spouse.

Based on the market for similar properties in your area, you believe you can rent the property for $1,200 per month. You have no mortgage on it, but you have the following annual expenses.

Property taxes	$2,800
Utilities	2,500
Insurance	700
Condo fees	1,800
Maintenance	600
Total	**8,400**

After consulting with us, you decide it would be in your best interest to file a U.S. tax return and take the deductions (file on a net basis) versus paying the withholding tax on gross rents.

Because you own the property jointly, both of you are required to obtain a U.S. Individual Tax Identification Number (ITIN) (discussed later in this chapter) and file a U.S. tax return. You are required to file Form 1040NR along with Schedule E by June 15th of the following tax year. Your U.S. tax filing position is summarized as follows.

U.S. (Florida) Rental Summary			
	Total $	You $	Spouse $
Gross Rents	14,000	7,200	7,200
Property Taxes	2,800	1,400	1,400
Utilities	2,500	1,250	1,250
Insurance	700	350	350
Condo Fees	1,800	900	900
Maintenance	600	300	300
Total Expenses	8,400	4,200	4,200
Depreciation*	7,273	3,637	3,637
Net Income/(Loss)	(1,273)	(637)	(637)

*Depreciation is a mandatory deduction for U.S. tax purposes and is determined by assuming $200,000 of the value of your Florida property is attributed to the building and the balance to the land, which is not depreciable. In the United States, residential real estate is depreciated on a straight-line basis with a life of 27.5 years ($7,273 = $200,000 / 27.5).

Although you have no tax liability in this example, you are still required to file a U.S. tax return and report the net rental loss of $637 on each of your respective U.S. federal returns (doing so will come in handy later on when you sell the property — see the next section).

You are also required to report and file the American rental activity in Canada on your personal T1 returns. Income and expenses need to be adjusted for Canadian dollars, and the use of the capital cost allowance (depreciation for U.S. purposes) is not mandatory for Canadian income tax purposes. Given that there is no U.S. tax due on the property, you would not be eligible to take a foreign tax credit on your Canadian return if you had a net profit (assuming you do not depreciate the Florida property for Canadian tax purposes).

Taxation of the Sale of U.S. Real Estate

We have had countless Canadians contact us wondering what the tax implications are when they sell their American properties. Many are confused about the U.S. tax withholding requirements and whether to file a tax return or not.

We had a client who sold a property in Arizona for a small U.S. gain. Under American rules, there is a requirement to withhold tax on the proceeds from the sale (discussed further in this chapter). However, the amount of withholding tax in this situation was significantly greater than the net tax on the capital gain. This individual was required and entitled to file a U.S. tax return reporting the capital gain and recovering his excess withholding tax. In this case, his expected refund due to the excess withholding was in the tens of thousands of dollars. However, because he and his spouse had failed to file Form 8840 — *Closer Connection Exception Statement for Aliens* for previous years, they were afraid that by filing a tax return the IRS would deny their refund. They were afraid of appearing on the IRS radar screen. Little did they know they were already on its radar screen — they had already withheld the required tax! We discussed the tax filing requirements applicable to them, put them at ease, and complied with those requirements. As a result, they got a big U.S. tax refund in American dollars! Surprisingly enough, these folks eventually retired in the United States permanently and hired us to help them with the planning for their transition there. Now these folks are definitely on the IRS radar screen!

U.S. Tax Implications

When selling American real estate, you are subject to U.S. income tax on the profit because the United States reserves the right to tax property within its borders. The profit is generally measured as the difference between the net proceeds from the sale and your cost base — referred to as "adjusted basis" in the United States. Your adjusted basis is the total of your purchase price plus the cost of permanent improvements less any U.S. depreciation taken (a mandatory deduction for U.S. tax purposes). If you previously failed to claim the appropriate depreciation, the IRS will generally reduce your adjusted basis as if you had claimed it.

If American real estate is held for longer than 12 months, the tax rate for individuals is generally a flat rate of 15%, except for the portion of the profit that represents "recaptured depreciation," which is taxed at 25%. If the real estate is held for less than 12 months, the regular U.S. graduated tax rates apply to any gain on the sale.

Form 1040NR must be filed by June 15th following the year of the sale *even if there was no profit on the sale!* You also need to include the American sale information on your Canadian income tax return, and this could lead to double taxation. This is where competent Canada-U.S. tax preparation can ensure that the tax paid in the United States is taken as a foreign tax credit on your Canadian return and that your tax is mitigated as much as possible. You also need to take into account currency gains and losses. As a result of currency fluctuations, the net realized capital gain or loss is different on the Canadian and American income tax returns. The adjusted cost base for

Canada needs to be adjusted to reflect the value of the U.S. dollar on the date of purchase. The sales proceeds also need to be adjusted to reflect the value of the U.S. dollar on the date of sale. If the American real estate sold is held on a joint basis, each spouse is required to file an American income tax return reporting one-half of the profit or loss on the return.

If you sell American property and have been a resident of Canada prior to September 27, 1980, you can likely take advantage of the Canada-U.S. Tax Treaty to reduce the gain. In such a case, only the gain accruing since January 1, 1985, will be taxed. To claim this benefit under the treaty, you need to make the claim when you file your U.S. tax return and include a statement containing specific information about the transaction. Note that this transitional rule does not apply to business properties that are part of a permanent establishment in the United States.

Under specific rules, American resident taxpayers might be able to defer the tax on the exchange of American real estate for other American real estate. However, this provision under the U.S. Internal Revenue Code (IRC) (known as a Section 1031 exchange) is not available to non-residents. We get numerous inquiries each year from Canadians who are told that they can defer the capital gains on their U.S. real estate under Section 1031. Unfortunately, the people telling you this likely don't realize you are a non-resident of the United States or don't fully understand American tax rules.

Furthermore, you are not able to exempt any realized gain if you were to buy another U.S. residence. The United States does have a $250,000 capital gains exemption per person ($500,000 per couple) and special tax rules for the sale of a principal residence. However, the American definition of "principal residence" is different from the definition used in Canada for Canadian income tax purposes. For U.S. income tax purposes, your principal residence is generally the residence you use the most. Therefore, it is difficult for most snowbirds to claim their American residence as their principal residence.

U.S. Withholding Tax on Real Estate Proceeds

In our experience, this is an area of great confusion and, if not dealt with properly, could cost you thousands of dollars and take plenty of time, effort, and professional fees to fix.

When you sell real estate in the United States, a tax of 10% of the gross sales price must normally be withheld by the buyer under the U.S. Foreign Investment in Real Property Tax Act of 1980 (FIRPTA) and remitted to the IRS. This withholding tax can be used to offset the actual U.S. income tax payable on any gain realized on the sale and is refunded if it exceeds the tax liability when you file your tax return. Depending on which state your property is located in, there may be state withholding requirements as well.

If your property sells for less than U.S.$300,000 to a buyer who intends to occupy the property as his or her residence, the 10% withholding tax on the sale proceeds doesn't apply. The buyer does not need to be an American citizen for this exception to apply; the only stipulation is that it will be his or her principal residence.

Another way to reduce the withholding tax requirements under FIRPTA is to apply to the IRS before the sale for an exemption. It applies only if the expected U.S. tax liability on the gain will be less than 10% of the sale proceeds. To do this, you file IRS Form 8288-B — *Application for Withholding Certificate for Dispositions by Foreign Persons of U.S. Real Property Interests*. If your application is accepted, the certificate will indicate the amount of tax that should be withheld by the buyer rather than the full 10%. This application must be filed with the IRS by the 20th day after the date of sale. Form 8288 along with the required withholding tax and copies A and B of Form(s) 8288-A should be mailed to

Internal Revenue Service,
Austin Service Center,
ITIN Operation,
Po Box 149342,
Austin, TX 78714-9342.

When you buy or sell American real estate, you need a U.S. Individual Taxpayer Identification Number (ITIN) to request the reduced withholding tax when selling the real estate and pay the requisite U.S. and/or state withholding tax. Information on obtaining an ITIN is discussed later in this chapter.

The IRS implemented new procedures effective December 17, 2003, to strengthen controls on the issue of ITINs. You are now required to file IRS Form W-7 — *Application for IRS Individual Taxpayer Identification Number* with Form 8288-B. To meet your closing date, you should file these forms six to eight weeks beforehand so that the withholding certificate is issued in time.

On Form W-7, either a request for an ITIN to pay FIRPTA withholding tax or a request for reduced FIRPTA withholding tax is made in box h, "Other," and is described as Exception 4 on page 3 of the instructions to Form W-7. To meet Exception 4, you check box h in the section of the form marked "Reason you are submitting Form W-7" and write "Exception 4" in the write-in area to the right of the box. The IRS issues ITINs only for applications that are complete and demonstrate a genuine need for an ITIN. Therefore, you should seek a competent Canada-U.S. advisor, or your Form 8288-B will not be processed, and the full 10% withholding tax will be withheld from your sale proceeds.

If you do not have a U.S. ITIN at the time of sale, two options are generally available to you:

(1) apply for the ITIN with Form 8288-B and 8288-A, and

(2) do not apply for an ITIN at the time of sale.

With the first option, you apply for an ITIN by filing Form W-7 (to be addressed later in this chapter) and attach it to Forms 8288-B and 8288-A. With the second option, generally most snowbirds do not have an ITIN (unless they have sold American property previously or have opened a U.S. bank account). This situation can cause a lot of confusion and lead to delays because, in our experience, most closing agents don't know how to deal with non-residents of the United States and the applicable IRS withholding tax and filing requirements. In this case, if Form 8288-A is submitted without an ITIN, the IRS will process the withholding tax payment and record it in your name (or names if held jointly). The form will be returned to you along with a letter stating the following:

> We are sending this letter to inform you that we are unable to mail your Form 8288-A, Statement of Withholding on Dispositions by Foreign Person of U.S. Real Property Interests (USRPI), because you did not supply us with your U.S. tax identification number (U.S. ITIN).
>
> Remember, the foreign transferor (seller) of the USRPI must have a U.S. ITIN in order to claim credit for the income tax withheld from the sale of the USRPI.

Although your processed and stamped Form 8288-A was not returned by the IRS, you are still able to file your U.S. income tax return and obtain a credit for the withholding tax. Just be sure to keep a copy of your Form 8288-A from the closing agent and attach it to your tax return. Remember, you still need to apply for an ITIN by filing and attaching Form W-7 to your tax return as well.

If you have sufficient lead time and your net capital gains tax is less than 10% of the gross proceeds (over U.S.$300,000), it is in your best interest to file an ITIN at the time you file Form 8288-B to reduce your withholding tax so that it is in line with the actual net U.S. tax you end up owing. If you don't, you are just giving the IRS an interest-free loan, which they won't mind at all.

Example of U.S. Withholding Tax under FIRPTA

Tom and Janet Snowbird are selling their winter home in Phoenix. They have been winter visitors to Phoenix for the past five years, but now with the birth of their first grandchild and

Tom's growing business they have decided to sell their Phoenix property so they can put the money into a cabin at Whistler, British Columbia.

They purchased the property four years ago for U.S.$350,000, and now they have an offer for U.S.$500,000. The Snowbirds are responsible for the capital gains tax calculated as $500,000 — $350,000 = $150,000. The current American long-term capital gains tax rate is 15%, so the amount of tax owing is $150,000 x 15% = $22,500 (before exemptions and other applicable deductions).

Under FIRPTA rules, property sales greater than U.S.$300,000 are automatically subject to a 10% withholding tax at closing. Because the withholding tax on $500,000 (10% = $50,000) is greater than the expected tax ($22,500), the Snowbirds should consider filing Form 8288-B to reduce the level of withholding tax. Ideally, this form is filed with the IRS before the date of closing to avoid the excess withholding tax. Regardless, the form must be filed with the IRS by the 20th day after the date of sale, or the mandatory 10% tax must be withheld. The Snowbirds can still recover the excess withholding tax by filing Form 1040NR. This return is due by June 15th in the year following the sale.

Example of Sale of U.S. Real Estate
Assumptions
- Emil and Ruth Canuck purchased an unfurnished condo for $200,000 in the United States in 2000 (owned jointly).
- They spent $20,000 on permanent improvements and $10,000 on furnishings.
- The property was never rented or used for business purposes.
- They sold the condo unfurnished in October of 2006 for $475,000.
- Upon the sale of the condo, they paid $14,100 in real estate commissions, $750 for a state transfer tax, and $1,400 for legal expenses and title work, for total expenses of $16,250.
- There was no mortgage on the property.

American Tax Implications

Their U.S. tax filing position is summarized as follows.

Because the property is held jointly, each spouse is taxed on one-half of the taxable amount ($117,675). The tax each spouse has to pay is $117,675 x 15% = $17,651. This means the total tax for both spouses is $35,303 (provided there are no other tax factors involved). Note that this does not include any applicable state taxes. States such as Hawaii and California impose a separate "state" income tax, while Florida, Texas, Washington, and Nevada don't have any state income tax.

Canadian Tax Implications

The Canucks are required to file a Canadian tax return and report the capital gain for Canadian purposes. Keep in mind that the capital gain calculation is different for Canadian tax purposes than for U.S. tax purposes. Also be aware of the potential additional gain or loss through foreign currency conversions based on the initial purchase price and the ultimate sale price.

Generally, any American capital gains tax paid on the profit

Selling Price		$475,000
Cost: Purchase Price	220,000	
Improvements	20,000	230,000
Profit		255,000
Selling Expenses		16,250
Capital Gain		238,750
Personal Exemption*		3,400
U.S. Taxable Amount		235,350
Amount of Gain for each spouse		117,675

*$3,400 is the allowable personal exemption amount given by the IRS for the 2007 tax year.

will be an eligible foreign tax credit for Canadian income tax purposes, eliminating all or most of the double taxation that can result in these transactions. Again, we highly recommend getting a Canada-U.S. tax expert to prepare these tricky tax returns to ensure that your tax liability is mitigated.

Obtaining a U.S. ITIN

As discussed above, if you have to file a U.S. income tax return because you rented or sold American real estate, you must have an Individual Taxpayer Identification Number (ITIN). An ITIN is often confused with a Social Security Number (SSN), but the two are completely different. SSNs are issued only to American citizens or U.S. residents who qualify for legal employment under certain visas. However, if you have ever been issued an SSN (let's say you previously worked or were a student in the United States), you should use that number instead. You should *never* use your Canadian Social Insurance Number (SIN) for U.S. tax filing purposes. In fact, under new rules enacted on December 17, 2003, the IRS now issues authorization letters instead of ITIN cards to avoid any possible similarities with U.S. Social Security cards.

Under the same rules, you need to show a federal tax purpose for having an ITIN. If you require an ITIN to meet your U.S. federal tax filing obligations for the sale or rental of American real estate, you are now required to attach IRS Form W-7 — *Application for IRS Individual Taxpayer Identification Number* (reproduced below) to the federal U.S. income tax return.

You may have to apply for an ITIN to report American interest income from a U.S. bank or investment account when the wrong withholding tax was taken. In this case, just provide evidence that you own the asset; you don't have to attach Form W-7 to your income tax return. There are 12 acceptable documents, including

(1) passport (if you submit an original valid passport or a notarized or certified copy of a valid passport, you don't need to submit any of the other documents listed below),

(2) national identity card (must show photo, name, current address, date of birth, and expiration date),

(3) American driver's license,

(4) civil birth certificate,

(5) foreign driver's license,

(6) U.S. state identification card,

(7) foreign voter's registration card,

(8) U.S. military identification card,

(9) visa for American immigration purposes,

(10) USCIS photo identification,

(11) medical records (dependents only), and

(12) school records (dependents and/or students only).

Copies are acceptable, but they must be certified. You can obtain certification of documents through an American consulate or through IRS-approved Certifying Acceptance Agents. Our firm is such an agent. A list of other firms or individuals that are Certified Acceptance Agents is available from the IRS website at www.irs.gov.

A completed Form W-7 with original or certified identity documentation and the required tax return should be mailed to

Internal Revenue Service
ITIN Operation
Po Box 149342
Austin, TX 78714-9342

If you were issued an ITIN prior to 1996, the IRS requires you to apply for a new one. An ITIN is for U.S. tax purposes only and doesn't permit you to work in the United States, give you immigration status there, or qualify you in any way for U.S. Social Security benefits.

If you, your spouse, or your dependent is an American citizen, national, resident alien, or person legally entitled to work in the United States, you are not eligible for an ITIN. Instead, you must apply for an SSN by filing Form SS-5 with the U.S. Social Security Administration (www.ssa.gov), not the IRS.

The normal processing time for an ITIN, according to the IRS, is between four and six weeks. However, in our experience, processing times are much longer, so we encourage you to submit Form W-7 well in advance of when you need it!

Taxation of U.S. Gambling Winnings

Many of you have spent some time in the casinos to take a break from the nice weather. Some of you have even hit the big jackpot but are shocked when the casino gives you a check for less than what you won. Snowbirds are subject to a tax on gambling or lottery winnings at the rate of 30% at the time of the win. However, this amount is not lost since there are two ways to get all, or at least some, of it back.

First, note that winnings from blackjack, baccarat, craps, roulette, and the "Big 6" wheel are exempt from U.S. tax. If you receive tax-exempt winnings from one of these games, or if the correct 30% withholding tax was collected at the time of winning, there is generally no requirement to file an American income tax return if this is your only U.S. income.

Second, keep in mind under the Canada-U.S. Tax Treaty that your gambling losses can be deducted from your winnings in the same calendar year. The same rules apply to American citizens and residents. For these reasons, we encourage you to keep an accurate record of any gambling winnings and losses using the following "recommendations" from the IRS.

1. Keep a diary of winnings and losses that contains

- the date and time of any specific wagering activity,
- the name and location of the gambling establishment and

Form **W-7**	**Application for IRS Individual Taxpayer Identification Number**	
(Rev. January 2007) Department of the Treasury Internal Revenue Service	▶ See instructions. ▶ For use by individuals who are not U.S. citizens or permanent residents.	OMB No. 1545-0074

An IRS individual taxpayer identification number (ITIN) is for federal tax purposes only.

FOR IRS USE ONLY

Before you begin:

- *Do not submit* this form if you have, or are eligible to obtain, a U.S. social security number (SSN).
- *Getting an ITIN does not change your immigration status or your right to work in the United States and does not make you eligible for the earned income credit.*

Reason you are submitting Form W-7. Read the instructions for the box you check. **Caution:** If you check box **b, c, d, e, f,** or **g,** you must file a tax return with Form W-7 unless you meet one of the exceptions (see instructions).

- a ☐ Nonresident alien required to obtain ITIN to claim tax treaty benefit
- b ☐ Nonresident alien filing a U.S. tax return
- c ☐ U.S. resident alien **(based on days present in the United States)** filing a U.S. tax return
- d ☐ Dependent of U.S. citizen/resident alien ⎤ Enter name and SSN/ITIN of U.S. citizen/resident alien (see instructions) ▶ ....
- e ☐ Spouse of U.S. citizen/resident alien ⎦ ....
- f ☐ Nonresident alien student, professor, or researcher filing a U.S. tax return or claiming an exception
- g ☐ Dependent/spouse of a nonresident alien holding a U.S. visa
- h ☐ Other (see instructions) ▶ ....
  Additional information for **a** and **f:** Enter treaty country ▶ .... and treaty article number ▶ ....

Name (see instructions)
Name at birth if different . . ▶

1a First name	Middle name	Last name
1b First name	Middle name	Last name

Applicant's mailing address

2 Street address, apartment number, or rural route number. **If you have a P.O. box, see page 4.**

City or town, state or province, and country. Include ZIP code or postal code where appropriate.

Foreign address (if different from above) (see instructions)

3 Street address, apartment number, or rural route number. **Do not use a P.O. box number.**

City or town, state or province, and country. Include ZIP code or postal code where appropriate.

Birth information

4 Date of birth (month / day / year) / /	Country of birth	City and state or province (optional)	5 ☐ Male ☐ Female

Other information

6a Country(ies) of citizenship	6b Foreign tax I.D. number (if any)	6c Type of U.S. visa (if any), number, and expiration date

6d Identification document(s) submitted (see instructions)
☐ Passport   ☐ Driver's license/State I.D.   ☐ USCIS documentation   ☐ Other ....
Issued by: No.:   Exp. date: /   /   Entry date in U.S.   /   /

6e Have you previously received a U.S. temporary taxpayer identification number (TIN) or employer identification number (EIN)?
☐ **No/Do not know.** Skip line 6f.
☐ **Yes.** Complete line 6f. If more than one, list on a sheet and attach to this form (see instructions).

6f Enter: TIN or EIN ▶ .... and
Name under which it was issued ▶

6g Name of college/university or company (see instructions) ....
City and state   Length of stay

Sign Here

Under penalties of perjury, I (applicant/delegate/acceptance agent) declare that I have examined this application, including accompanying documentation and statements, and to the best of my knowledge and belief, it is true, correct, and complete. I authorize the IRS to disclose to my acceptance agent returns or return information necessary to resolve matters regarding the assignment of my IRS individual taxpayer identification number (ITIN), including any previously assigned taxpayer identifying number.

Keep a copy for your records.

Signature of applicant (if delegate, see instructions) ▶	Date (month / day / year) / /	Phone number
Name of delegate, if applicable (type or print)	Delegate's relationship to applicant ▶	☐ Parent ☐ Court-appointed guardian ☐ Power of Attorney

Acceptance Agent's Use ONLY

Signature ▶	Date (month / day / year) / /	Phone ( ) Fax ( )
Name and title (type or print) ▶	Name of company	EIN EFIN/Office Code

For Paperwork Reduction Act Notice, see page 4.   Cat. No. 10229L   Form **W-7** (Rev. 1-2007)

the table number,
- the names of other persons present with you, and
- *all* amounts *won and lost.*

2. Keep all wagering tickets — keno, unredeemed lottery ticket, racetrack, bingo card — and costs such as

- canceled checks,
- credit card records relating to withdrawals of gambling funds,
- casino credit records,
- bank withdrawals,
- statement(s) of actual winnings provided by the gambling establishment (IRS Form[s] 1042-S, W2-G, and 5754), and
- casino "play" records that you may be able to request.

For U.S. tax filing purposes, you need a complete record of your reported and unreported winnings to net the two together. The regulations state, in effect, *no records, no deductions!* Again, you need to obtain an ITIN before filing any U.S. income tax return.

Example

Gladys, a snowbird who winters in Sun City, Arizona, makes a trip to Laughlin, Nevada, to "play the slots." She finds the "slot gods" are kind to her that day, and she ends up winning U.S.$4,800. However, she gets a check for only $3,360 and then realizes that 30% of her winnings ($1,440) has been sent to the IRS. It appears the "tax gods" are also hanging around that day. Is Gladys able to recover any of the American withholding tax from her win? Because she read this book, she has been faithfully documenting all of her gambling activities this year and has evidence to support $1,800 in losses. Gladys applies for an ITIN and files a tax return to get $540 back ($4,800 — $1,800 = $3,000 x 30% = $900 less $1,440 overwithheld = $540 refund!).

U.S. Withholding Tax Recovery Firms

A number of firms in Canada will be happy to help you recover your withholding tax from gambling winnings in the United States. Essentially, what they do is what you could do yourself: apply for an ITIN and file Form 1040NR to recover the American withholding tax.

For providing this service, these firms are paid a percentage of the refunds they recover. For example, many firms charge 30% of the refund for amounts up to U.S.$2,000, 25% for amounts between U.S.$2,000 and $5,000, and 20% for amounts over U.S.$5,000. Ultimately, it is up to you to evaluate the cost versus the benefit of this service. Many Canadians believe that using these firms might guarantee or expedite receiving excess American withholding taxes. However, nothing could be further from the truth. You still have to go through the normal routine of getting an ITIN (four to six weeks) and then filing your tax return provided you have documented your losses sufficiently. In our opinion, doing the work yourself or using a national or local accounting firm that charges only for time is a much better deal.

U.S. Tax Scam Directed at Unsuspecting Snowbirds

With the advent of computer technology, identity theft is becoming a greater concern for all consumers these days. Over the past number of years, a scam has been perpetuated out of the United States aimed at unsuspecting snowbirds. This scam aims to get your confidential personal, financial, and banking information for your accounts in the United States.

A letter (note the misspelling and inconsistent capitalization in the original), supposedly from the "Director of Information" — a Mr. Jerry Green — of the United State of America Internal Revenue Services, requests that recipients complete Form W-8Ben11, Certification of foreign status Beneficiary Owner for United States of America Tax withholding, in order to protect their exemption from U.S. income tax and withholding tax on U.S. bank interest earned by a non-resident alien. The letter includes a fax number and requests that Form W8-Ben11 be returned within one week of receipt.

Upon first glance, you should note that the letterhead indicates the United "State" of America as opposed to the United "States" of America. As well, it indicates the Internal Revenue "Services" as opposed to the legitimate Internal Revenue "Service."

Form W-8Ben11 is a *false* form, never produced by the U.S. Department of Treasury or the IRS. The form accompanying the letter is designed to look very similar to IRS Form W8-BEN, a legitimate form used by American withholding agents and financial institutions to ensure that accounts are eligible for a reduced American withholding tax as opposed to having 30% tax withheld from accounts. In fact, this form does not have to be filed with the IRS but is kept on file with the U.S. withholding agent and/or financial institution. The bogus W-8Ben11 form asks a number of personal questions (passport number, mother's maiden name, bank account numbers, arrival and departure dates, etc.) that are not on the legitimate IRS Form W-8BEN.

If you receive such a form or anything like it, *do not complete it* without first checking with your American financial institution. You may also want to notify your financial institution as well as your Canadian and/or U.S. tax advisor or closest American consulate so that various associations, financial institutions, and government agencies can be notified.

Additional Tips

- Keep track of the number of days that you are in the United States so that this information is available for IRS Form 8840 or page 5 of IRS Form 1040NR.
- If you will be out of Canada on April 30th, make sure your tax preparer has everything required to prepare and file your Canadian tax return.
- If eligible to do so, make your RRSP contribution prior to leaving Canada during the winter months.

3

A Home Away from Home

Purchasing U.S. Real Estate

In Chapter 2, we discussed the U.S. income tax implications of the rental or sale of American real estate. However, the majority of inquiries from snowbirds at our firm surrounds the purchase and titling of U.S. real estate by Canadian residents. It is important to be aware of the process for acquiring American real estate, for improper ownership can result in adverse Canadian and American income, gift, and estate tax consequences (further discussion of the estate planning issues is presented in Chapter 5). Based on your specific financial situation, you might be lucky enough to acquire your "home away from home" through your own financial resources. If this isn't the case, you'll likely require a mortgage.

American and Canadian Mortgage Differences

There are huge differences in mortgages between Canada and

the United States, and they clearly favor the latter country. Since buying a home is typically the largest single purchase most people make in their lifetimes, getting the right mortgage should be of primary consideration. Our firm has helped numerous clients to obtain the right mortgage with the right terms from the right broker and/or financial institution.

As in Canada, in the United States real estate transactions are generally formalized through a written agreement referred to as a "Contract for Sale and Purchase." This document is jointly signed by the buyer and seller and generally details the terms of the transaction, including purchase and sale price, related expenses, and closing date. Unlike in Canada, though, in the United States most real estate transactions are completed through a title insurance or escrow agent who organizes and conducts the closing on behalf of the buyer and seller. It is rare that a lawyer is involved in U.S. real estate transactions involving personal residences.

Expenses for a real estate transaction in the United States generally include legal fees, real estate commissions, prorated property tax and mortgage interest costs, transfer taxes, title insurance costs, homeowner or condo association fees, and document recording fees. A buyer in the United States is generally required to obtain title insurance to confirm clear title to the property, and we recommend it as a good idea. If the title history of the property becomes unclear and the legitimate owner steps forward, you could lose your property or be forced to pay the legitimate owner the fair price for it.

At sale closing, the title or escrow agent will generally send a new title certificate or deed to the state county recorder's office to record the new legal title to the property.

Amortization

In Canada, the typical mortgage is amortized over 25 years, while it is 15 or 30 years in the United States. Taking a 30-year mortgage will obviously lower your monthly payments from those of a 15-year mortgage, but which mortgage you select depends on your individual circumstances. There are a number of other loan options (e.g., adjustable rate and shorter fixed rate terms) to consider, and they may better suit your situation.

Fixed Interest Rate

In Canada, the typical mortgage fixes your interest rate for up to 10 years, and then it is adjusted to the prevailing rate at that time. You are required to bear the risk of any interest rate changes. This is where a U.S. mortgage has a big advantage over those in Canada, because you can fix your interest rate for the full 15- or 30-year amortization — the bank bears the interest rate risk. This fixed rate can make a huge difference in stabilizing one of your largest debts over the long term. The other nice thing with mortgages in the United States is that, if rates decline significantly at any point, you can refinance your mortgage and lock it in for another 15 or 30 years, lowering your monthly payments even further. In addition, mortgages in the United States use simple interest calculations, while in Canada interest is compounded semi-annually. This means you will pay more interest in the United States if you make the minimum payment for the entire term of the mortgage, but you will pay less if you ever get in arrears because there is no interest on the interest, as there is in Canada. Likewise, U.S. lenders will typically charge a late fee for payments made in arrears, while these fees are typically prohibited in Canada.

Unlike in Canada (unless you are self-employed and are using part of your home as an office), mortgage interest may be "deductible" for income tax purposes in the United States. However, unless you are a U.S. income tax resident (citizen or green card holder) or rent out your American property, you will derive no U.S. income tax benefit from the interest you pay on your U.S. mortgage. However, we have seen pronouncements from some advisors to "deduct your U.S. mortgage interest in Canada." They are recommending to their clients that they obtain a mortgage against their U.S. property, invest the proceeds with them, and deduct the interest costs on their Canadian tax return against the investment income generated from the mortgage proceeds. This is a legitimate strategy, but it's an important financial decision that needs to be balanced against your overall objectives, risk tolerance, and any perceived conflicts of interest imposed by the advisor managing these proceeds. This is a concept called leverage, and it works well when the leveraged investment is increasing in value. However, we all know that what goes up must eventually come down, so the effects of leverage work in the opposite direction as well and could force some cash flow hardship that hopefully you have planned for.

Prepayments

This is another area that makes American mortgages far superior to Canadian mortgages. Most U.S. mortgages have no prepayment penalties, while Canadian financial institutions typically impose penalties for prepayments, restrict them to the loan anniversary, or simply don't allow prepayments at all. In the United States, you can send in as much additional money above your monthly mortgage payment as you wish, and it all gets applied to the principal. This means you can pay off your mortgage whenever you have the funds to do so. However, be wary and make sure you get a conventional mortgage.

Many Canadians often want to set up biweekly payment schedules on their American mortgages because it is an effective strategy in Canada to pay off your mortgage sooner. In the United States, you have to be careful: U.S. financial institutions are often happy to oblige because there are many hidden costs and fees, and this approach typically doesn't make sense because you can accomplish the same thing by making an extra payment per year on your mortgage.

Down Payment

To purchase a home in Canada, you are required to put 25% or more down to avoid paying for mortgage insurance from the Canada Mortgage and Housing Corporation (CMHC). In the United States, the requirement is only 20% to avoid paying for mortgage insurance from the Federal Housing Authority (FHA) or a private insurer such as Fannie Mae. Depending on your situation, there are ways of structuring your mortgage to avoid the mortgage insurance while putting less than 20% down.

Closing Costs

It has been our experience that closing costs in Canada are typically higher than those in the United States. In particular, lender fees in the United States are around U.S.$400 versus C$1,000 in Canada. In addition, legal fees and land title fees are part of the closing costs in Canada but not in the United States. Typically, however, you don't need a termite inspection fee in Canada! The other difference when closing on a house in Canada is that you typically use an attorney to handle the transaction. As mentioned above, in the United States you use a title company almost exclusively to complete the transaction, and title insurance is a good thing.

Points

You'll see "points" only in the United States, and they can offer substantial benefits if planned correctly. There are three types of points: discount points, loan origination points, and seller paid points. Discount points allow you to "buy down" the interest rate on your mortgage. A point is typically one percent of the loan amount and can reduce your interest rate by one-eighth or so. This system gives you more flexibility in creating a mortgage that works for you. Origination points, on the other hand, are fees charged by the lender for the evaluation, preparation, and submission of your mortgage loan application (typically "junk" fees). There are also seller paid points to provide an incentive to buyers by offering a discount of a certain percentage on the sale of a home. For you, points paid can often be deductible for U.S.

income tax purposes upon the sale of the American property. Be wary of mortgage companies that announce they have "no fees, no closing costs," on their mortgages. These folks are not in the mortgage business because they want to lose money or break even. They make money and just hide the costs in a higher interest rate, so be sure to shop around and get a few "good faith estimates" from those financial institutions you are considering.

Impound (Escrow) Accounts

Impound accounts are another item seen only in the United States. The mortgage lender will automatically roll your homeowner insurance and property taxes into your monthly payment so they can be "precollected." The insurance company or local municipality sends the bill directly to the mortgage company, which pays the money out of your "escrow/impound account." The rationale behind these accounts is that, since the mortgage company owns 80% or more of the U.S. home, it can legally ensure that the property taxes are paid and the home is protected in the event of fire or some other catastrophe. The company collects the money for these items in advance as part of your monthly mortgage payment and earns interest on it until the money is due. Overall, if you have more than 20% equity in your home, these accounts are generally a bad deal for you because it's like making an interest-free loan to your mortgage company. Interestingly enough, in most cases, the mortgage company doesn't discuss this with you or give you the option beforehand, so ask some questions and be wary before accepting these impositions.

Obtaining a U.S. Mortgage

In qualifying for a mortgage in the United States, things can get a little tricky given that you don't have a credit rating there. Regardless of what your financial position or credit worthiness back in Canada is, most U.S. banks and mortgage companies might not be in a position to assist you. Banks often "pass" on the opportunity to finance your American real estate purchase because you don't file U.S. income tax returns, don't have a U.S. Social Security Number, and/or don't have a U.S. credit record or bureau file.

Be prepared, then, to provide appropriate documentation to a U.S. lender. In many cases, this documentation is not easily available to a U.S. lender. For that reason, you might want to obtain your own credit bureau file in Canada to take to the United States in anticipation of applying for a mortgage.

There are two Canadian credit-reporting agencies that you can contact: Equifax Canada (1-800-465-7166, 514-493-2314, or www.econsumer.equifax.ca), and TransUnion (1-800-663-9980 or www.tuc.ca). With this information along with a letter from your Canadian bank manager, your Canadian passport, and your financial and income statements and Canadian tax returns, you might be in a better position to approach U.S. financial institutions or mortgage brokers to obtain mortgage financing tailored to your needs.

A number of U.S. financial institutions have seen snowbirds as a good business opportunity and have created banking and lending services for them. In this case, you might want to work through a lender that knows and has the ability to access your credit bureau file from Canada. One lender that has mortgage programs specifically designed for Canadians is RBC Centura Bank, part of RBC Financial Group. Its Cross Border Mortgage Program (www.rbcroyalbank.com/usbanking/rbc-access-usa.html) allows it to access your credit file in Canada and package a mortgage solution for you.

Finally, be aware of the impact of a fluctuating Canadian loonie against a fixed U.S. dollar mortgage payment as part of your overall planning decision. See Chapter 4 for further information.

Common U.S. Real Estate Terms

There are a number of new terms you should be familiar with when purchasing a U.S. property and a mortgage.

- *Escrow agent:* The closing of a transaction through a third party called an escrow agent, which receives certain funds and documents to be delivered upon the performance of certain conditions outlined in the escrow instructions.
- *Title insurance:* A policy insuring the owner against loss by reason of defects in the title to a parcel of real estate, other than encumbrances, defects, and matters specifically excluded by the policy.
- *Certificate of title:* A statement of opinion on the status of the title to a parcel of real estate based on an examination of specified public records.
- *Closing statement:* A detailed cash accounting of a real estate transaction showing all cash received, all charges and credits made, and all cash paid out in the transaction.
- *Deed:* A written instrument that, when executed and delivered, conveys title to or an interest in real estate.
- *Escrow account:* The trust account established for the purpose of holding funds on behalf of the real estate parties until the consummation or termination of the real estate transaction.
- *Homeowner's insurance policy:* A standardized insurance policy that covers a residential real estate owner against financial loss from fire, theft, public liability, and other common risks.
- *Listing agreement:* A contract between an owner (as principal) and a real estate broker (as agent) by which the broker is employed to find a buyer for the owner's real estate on the owner's terms, for which service the owner may agree to pay a commission.
- *Quitclaim deed:* A conveyance by which the grantor transfers whatever interest he or she has in the real estate, without warranties or obligations.
- *Conveyance:* Any document that transfers title to real estate. The term is also used to describe the act of transferring.
- *Recording:* The act of entering or recording documents

affecting or conveying interests in real estate in the recorder's office established in each county. Until it is recorded, a deed or mortgage is ordinarily not effective against subsequent purchasers or mortgagees.

- *Transfer tax:* Tax stamps that need to be affixed to a deed by state and/or local law.
- *Settlement charges:* Summary of the disclosure of costs and expenses of the buyer and seller. Typically provided by the title company in the United States.

Ways to Own and/or Title U.S. Real Estate

As discussed above, the ownership of real estate can have Canadian and American income, gift, and estate tax implications for the owners of the property. Ownership can also create benefits and consequences from an estate planning perspective, depending on the intentions of the owners. It's therefore critical that you understand the implications of titling any U.S. property you own.

Sole and Separate

This is individual ownership of property by a person. At death, the decedent's will governs the ultimate distribution of the real estate held this way. If the decedent dies without a will (intestate), the laws of the state where the property is held govern to whom the real estate ultimately goes and how this transfer occurs.

Joint Tenancy

This is generally the most common form of ownership of real estate between spouses and family members. *Barron's Dictionary of Legal Terms* defines joint tenancy as "A single estate in property, real or personal, owned by two or more persons, under one instrument or act of the parties, with an equal right in all to share in the enjoyment during their lives. On the death of a joint tenant, the property descends to the survivor or survivors and at length to the last survivor." Upon the death of a joint tenant, the decedent's interest passes to the surviving joint tenant or tenants by the right of survivorship, also known as joint tenancy with rights of survivorship (JTWROS). Because this form of title passes by law, it doesn't matter what your will says or what your intentions might be: property titled this way will pass to the surviving joint tenant at death. Also be aware that, although property might be titled this way, it might not be accepted as such for U.S. gift and estate tax considerations (see Chapter 5 for further information).

Community Property

This system of property ownership is based on the theory that each spouse has an equal interest in the property acquired by the efforts of either spouse during marriage and is not available in all states. Community property snowbird states include Arizona and California.

Tenancy in Common

This is a form of co-ownership in which each owner holds an undivided interest in real estate as if he or she were the sole owner. Each owner has the right to partition. Unlike joint tenants, tenants in common have the right of inheritance, so the decedent's will governs where you want your interest to go at your death. There can be some U.S. gift and estate tax benefits if property is held this way (see Chapter 5 for further information).

Corporations, Trusts, Partnerships

In some cases, lawyers and accountants might suggest that you hold property in a Canadian corporation, trust, or partnership. In other cases, they might suggest that you hold your American property in a U.S. or foreign trust. Generally, the logic behind owning property this way is to minimize or eliminate U.S. estate tax. Although owning property through an entity might remove the property for U.S. estate tax purposes, if you are using the property personally, the structure that holds the property could be attacked as a sham under American rules. Furthermore, the income tax consequences upon the sale of a property owned by an entity would be subject to U.S. tax rates as high as 39% as opposed to the lower capital gains rate of 15% if held personally. Also, the practical constraints imposed on you when you own property this way can be an administrative burden. For further information on the ways to reduce, defer, or eliminate estate tax on U.S. property, see Chapter 5.

4

Money Doesn't Grow on Trees

Money Management for Snowbirds

Unfortunately for many snowbirds, the value of the Canadian loonie against the U.S. dollar dictates whether and for how long they spend time in the United States. In the past when the dollar was much lower, many of you put off your travel plans, praying for the dollar to regain some of its strength. The value of the dollar and the ever-increasing costs of health care and travel insurance comprise a tricky set of variables that have to be considered for a successful snowbird lifestyle.

Each year over 1.5 million Canadians go south for the winter. In most cases, they spend a minimum of two months in the United States. Given the limited banking choices in Canada relative to those south of the border, some of the major Canadian banks have recognized the needs of Canadian customers while they are in the United States and have developed products and services geared specifically toward them. Amazingly enough, most U.S. banks don't offer Canadian loonie accounts or seem to be unwilling to accommodate temporary residents in the United States.

Over the past few years, some Canadian banks have made significant inroads across the line through the acquisition of U.S. banks. They include the Royal Bank of Canada with its purchase of RBC Centura, TD Canada Trust with its purchase of TD Banknorth, and the Bank of Montreal with its purchase of Harris Bank.

U.S. Banking for Snowbirds

Following is a summary of some of the banking services you can have as a customer of a Canadian bank while down south.

Royal Bank of Canada

With its purchase of RBC Centura a number of years ago, the Royal Bank of Canada (RBC) appears to have the best banking packages, referred to as Access USA accounts, for snowbirds in the United States. See chart on following page.

Through its Cross Border Mortgage Program, RBC Centura is able to obtain Canadian credit bureau files to coordinate the financing requirements of Canadians in the United States. RBC Centura branches are located in Florida, Georgia, North Carolina, South Carolina, and Virginia, but its mortgage services are available in most states.

For further information on RBC Centura's banking program for Canadians, go to www.rbccentura.com/personal/snowbirds/main.html.

Bank of Montreal

The Bank of Montreal (BMO) is affiliated with Harris Bank in the United States. BMO has four kinds of banking plans, with the Premium Plan providing for U.S. dollar requirements. The monthly banking fee is $25, while the minimum monthly balance needed to eliminate the fee is $4,500.

Service	Access USA Preferred Service	Access USA Service
	Monthly fee waived with a U.S.$5,000 minimum monthly checking balance, minimum U.S.$10,000 total deposit balance, or U.S.$20,000 combined balance of deposits and credit line or just U.S.$29.95 per month	Monthly fee waived with a U.S.$700 minimum monthly balance or U.S.$3.95 per month
RBC Centura U.S. Checking Account	**Preferred Checking Account**	**Royal Embassy Checking Account**
	Free ATM card Free wallet-style checks No-charge checking Interest-bearing account Unlimited teller transactions	Free ATM card Free wallet-style checks No-charge checking Interest-bearing account Unlimited teller transactions
RBC Centura Web Banking and U.S. Bill Payment	Included	Included
Travellers Checks	Commission free	Standard rates/fees apply
Safe Deposit Box	No-charge small safe deposit box at a local RBC Centura location	Standard rates/fees apply
Foreign Exchange	Preferred rate on instant money transfers and for purchase or sale of U.S. funds in Canada	Standard rates/fees apply
Instant Online Money Transfers	Unlimited between RBC Royal Bank and RBC Centura	Unlimited between RBC Royal Bank and RBC Centura
ATM Access	No charge at RBC Centura/Publix ATMs or other ATMs, plus fees charged by other banks are rebated (up to four per month)	No charge at RBC Centura/Publix ATMs; up to two $2 ATM rebates per month
RBC Royal Bank U.S.$ VISA Gold	Fee waived annually for primary and co-applicant Earns RBC rewards points Transactions in U.S. funds to avoid daily currency fluctuations	Not included
Optional Travel Insurance	Extensive insurance Preferred rates	Competitively priced

In the United States, you are limited to five monthly debit transactions using non-BMO ATMs on the Cirrus network. Furthermore, your direct purchases in the United States using the Maestro service cannot exceed five per month. This plan provides preferred exchange rates on up to U.S.$5,000 per transaction. U.S. dollar bill payments and transfers to American financial institutions through telephone banking are also part of this service.

A unique cash management tool exclusively available through BMO is its Prepaid Travel Mosaik MasterCard. Introduced in June 2007, the card is a viable — but more expensive — alternative to traveler's checks. BMO customers can "fill up" the card with cash and use it like a regular MasterCard to make purchases or withdrawals from an ATM. For safety purposes, if you lose the card, it can be canceled and the funds replaced. Although this can be a practical alternative to cash or traveler's checks when traveling, it does come with a steep price. The annual card fee is C$9.95 — an additional C$9.95 will be charged if you want a card for your spouse or another family member. If you use the card at an ATM outside Canada and in the United States, you'll be charged C$4.50 per transaction. Furthermore, there is a foreign currency markup of 2.5% on top of the currency exchange rate. Despite the high fees to use the card, you do receive one air mile point for every C$40 you spend with the card.

The enCircle Eldercare Service provides referrals to snowbird services; effectively, this is an introduction to a representative of Harris Bank in the United States. In terms of the needs of snowbirds, Harris Bank has branches in Florida and Arizona. For further information on BMO Harris Private Banking and Harris Bank's banking program for Canadians, check www.bmo-harrisprivatebanking.com/enCircle/whatisencircle.asp and www4.harrisbank.com/.

TD Canada Trust

TD has a specific account, called its Borderless Plan, tailored to customers who spend time in or travel to the United States. This is a U.S. dollar checking/savings account. The monthly fee is U.S.$4.95 but is waived if you maintain a minimum monthly balance of U.S.$3,000.

There are no fees on U.S. dollar transactions, including checks, withdrawals, bill payments, and transfers through Interac, PLUS, and NYCE debit networks. TD charges no commissions to obtain U.S. dollar traveler's checks. It also gives customers preferred exchange rates on amounts up to U.S. $25,000. Furthermore, TD provides travel medical insurance, and Borderless Plan holders receive a five percent discount on this insurance.

TD Banknorth has branches throughout the northeastern United States. For further information on TD Canada Trust and TD Banknorth, go to www.tdcanadatrust.com/accounts/borderless.jsp and www.tdbanknorth.com.

Canadian Imperial Bank of Commerce

CIBC is the only major Canadian bank that no longer has any affiliated banking in the United States. However, it does have a U.S. dollar Personal Account available to customers who travel or spend time in the United States.

Other than its travel insurance plan, CIBC has very limited banking options for customers in the United States compared with the other major banks. It provides the opportunity to deposit U.S. currency in or withdraw it from specific U.S. currency bank machines.

For further information on CIBC's U.S. dollar Personal Account, see www.cibc.com/ca/chequing-savings/us-personal-acct.html.

National Bank of Canada

The National Bank of Canada has no affiliated bank in the United States and provides only a U.S. dollar account for customers who travel to or spend time in the United States. Its

Progress Account is available for U.S. dollars and provides savings on fees and transaction costs with a minimum monthly balance of U.S.$2,500. For further information on the National Bank's U.S. dollar Progress Account, check www.nbc.ca/bnc/-cda/content/0,1008,divId-2_langId-1_navCode-10029,00.html.

Scotiabank

Scotiabank does not have a direct U.S. affiliated bank. However, it's the founding member of the Global ATM Alliance, which allows its customers to withdraw cash at likely the highest number of ATM providers without any access fees. The U.S. member of the Global ATM Alliance is the Bank of America, which has over 16,600 ATMs throughout the United States.

For Scotia customers who spend time in or travel to the U.S., they have access to a U.S. dollar Daily Interest Account. It appears that, of all the major Canadian banks, Scotia has the lowest monthly account fee for a U.S. dollar account. It has no monthly fee as long as you maintain a minimum monthly balance of U.S.$200. However, that includes only two transactions (checks, preauthorized payments, cash withdrawals, and teller-assisted account transfers). Additional transactions are U.S.$0.60 each, and if the daily account balance drops below U.S.$200 a monthly maintenance fee of a dollar is imposed. The account does provide commission-free U.S. dollar money orders and traveler's checks.

Although Scotia doesn't have a package specifically tailored to snowbirds, it does have a program for seniors that includes a U.S. dollar Daily Interest Savings Account. The account also bundles six other accounts (Scotia Powerchequing, Basic Banking, Daily Interest Savings, Scotia U.S. Dollar Daily Interest Savings, Scotia Gain Plan Investment Savings Account, and Money Matter High Interest Savings Account). This account has no monthly fees and provides up to 40 transactions without a fee. Beyond the 40 transactions, a fee of c$0.65 is imposed.

For further information on Scotiabank's U.S. dollar Daily

Interest Savings Account and Scotia Plus Program for seniors, go to www.scotiabank.com/cda/content/0,1608,CID484_LIDen,-00.htm or www.scotiabank.com/cda/content/0,1608,CID483_LIDen,00.html.

HSBC Canada

HSBC, which dubs itself "the world's local bank," has affiliated branches in the northeastern United States in addition to branches in Washington, Oregon, California, and Florida. HSBC Canada has a U.S. dollar account bundled with its regular Canadian dollar checking and savings accounts for customers over the age of 60. It's called the Performance 60 Account. Its features include

- no monthly administration fee,
- no monthly fee for Internet banking,
- 12 free in-branch debit transactions, checks, and electronic transactions per month plus one free debit each month for each automated credit processed to the account,
- free in-branch bill payments,
- free telephone banking-assisted bill payments or account transfers,
- a rebate on a safe deposit box, and
- interest calculated on the daily closing balance paid monthly.
- (Includes telephone banking, Internet banking, Interac, direct payment, HSBC Canada and Exchange abm debit transactions, and preauthorized/electronic debit transactions.)

For further information on HSBC's Power 60 Account and banking services abroad, check www.hsbc.ca/hsbc/personal_en/accounts/performance-chequing/performance-60 and www.hsbc.ca/hsbc/ personal_en/travel/retiring-abroad.

ATB Financial

A banking network serving Alberta exclusively, ATB provides a

U.S. dollar Savings Account for customers without a monthly fee or minimum balance requirement. For further information on its U.S. dollar Savings Account, check www.atb.com/Dev/accounts/accounts_usdollar.asp.

Desjardins

This banking network serves Quebec, New Brunswick, Manitoba, and Ontario. Its Build-Up Savings Account provides banking and checking transactions in U.S. dollars. No monthly fee is imposed on this account as long as the minimum monthly balance is U.S.$1,000. For further information on this account, see www.desjardins.com/en/particuliers/produits_services/comptes_frais/comptes.jsp#ame.

NYCE Payments Network

The NYCE Payments Network connects more than 2,429 financial institutions with more than 280,000 ATMs and more than 1.5 million point-of-sale locations in the U.S., providing consumers with secure, real-time access to their money anywhere and anytime they need it.

The following Canadian banks are part of the NYCE network.

- RBC Royal Bank
- National Bank of Canada
- Scotia Bank
- Desjardins
- TD Canada Trust
- ATB Financial

NYCE gives Canadians the ability to use their ATM bank cards through a large number of alternative bank ATMs and many U.S. retailers. My RBC debit card has been slightly abused by my many Arizona Costco visits using the NYCE service. My transaction fee is C$0.75 each time I use my RBC debit card through an NYCE U.S. retailer.

Following is a list of the major retailers in the United States where you can use your Canadian bank debit card.

Major Retailers that Accept NYCE for Purchases

Apparel and Accessories	
Abercrombie & Fitch	Journeys
Ann Taylor*	Marty Shoes
Babies R US	Old Navy
Banana Republic*	Pacific Sunwear*
Bob's Stores	Parade of Shoes
Burlington Coat Factory	Payless Shoe Stores
Champs	Rainbow Appare
Chico's	S&K Famous Brands
Children's Place*	Talbots
DSW	The Finish Line
Fashion Bug	The Shoe Dept
Foot Action USA	The Sports Authority
Foot Locker	TJ Maxx
Gap*	Urban Outfitters
Hat World	Van's
J Crew	
Department Stores	
Belik	L.S. Ayres
Bloomingdale's	Macy's
Dillards	Marshalls
Famous-Barr	Meier & Frank
Filene's	Mervyn's
Foley's	Nordstrom
Hechts	Rich's
The Jones Store	Robinsons-May
Kaufmanns	Ross Stores
Kohl's	Sears

Lazarus	Value City
Lord & Taylor	

Discount/Wholesale Clubs

Bigg's	Ocean State Job Lot
BJ's Wholesale Club	Sam's Club
Costco	Save-A-Lot
Cub Foods	ShopKo Stores
Dollar General*	Super K-Mart
Dollar Tree*	Target
Family Dollar*	Wal-Mart
K-Mart	

Hardware/Home Improvement Stores

Ace Hardware*	Lowes
ACo Hardware	Menards
Home Depot	

Gas/Convenience Stores

7-Eleven	Merit Gas Stations
76 Gasoline	Mobil
Amoco	Quick Chek
BP Gasoline	QuikTrip (QT)
Chevron	Race Trac
Circle K*	Red Apple Markets
Citgo Gasoline*	Sheetz*
Cumberland Farms*	Shell Gasoline
Dairy Mart	Sunoco
Exxon	Texaco
Getty Gasoline	Thornton Oil
Gulf Oil	Turkey Hill Markets*
Hess Gasoline	Wawa*
Kum & Go	Wilson Farms
KWIK Fill	

Drugstores

Bartell Drugs	Kinney Drugs
Brooks Pharmacy	Long Drugs
CVS Pharmacy	Maxi Drugs

Duane Reade, Inc.	Osco Drug
Eckerd Drugs	Rite Aid
Kerr Drugs	Walgreens
Supermarkets/Grocery Stores	
A&P	Kroger
Acme Markets	Marsh's Supermarket
Albertson's	Mayfair Supermarkets
Aldi Food Stores	Meijer
Associated Foods	P&C
Bashas'	Pathmark
Big Y	Pick 'n Save
Binghamton Giant Market	Piggly Wiggly*
Bread & Circus	Price Chopper
Brookshire Brothers	Publix SuperMarkets
C-Town*	Purity
D'Agostino	Quality Markets
Dean & Deluca	Rainbow Stores
Demoula Market Basket	Raleys
Dillons Stores*	Ralph's Grocery
Dominick's	Reasors
Eagle Food Centers	Redners Warehouse
Edwards	Roche Brothers
Farm Fresh*	Ro-Jacks
Farmer Jack	Safeway
Fisher Foods	Schnucks Market
Food Emporium	Scott's
Food Lion*	Shaw's
Food Mart*	Shop Rite
Foodmaster*	Shop-N-Save*
Foodtown	Slater Bros
Fred Meyer	Spartan Stores
Fresh Fields	Star Markets
Genuardi's	Stew Leonard's
Giant Eagle	Stop & Shop
Giant Foods	Super Fresh

Gristede's	SUPERVALU*
Hannaford Brothers	Tops Markets
Harris Teeter	Trader Joe's
H-E-B Grocery	V.G.'s Food
Hy-Vee, Inc.	Victory Markets
InglesWaldbaum's	Wegmans
Insalaco's	Weis Markets
Jewel Food	Western Beef
Jubiliee*	Whole Foods Market*
Key Food*	Wild Oats
King Kullen	Winn Dixie Stores
King Soopers	
King Supermarket	
Restaurants*	
A&W	KFC
Chili's	Long John Silver's
Chuck E Cheese	McDonald's
Del Taco	Subway
Great American	Taco Bell
Other Retail Stores	
Alco	HomeGoods
Army Airforce Exchange Services	IKEA
Auto Zone	Kirklands
Barnes & Noble	Linens & Things
Bed Bath & Beyond	Michaels
BestBuy	Office Depot
Blockbuster	Video Petco
Brookstone	PetSmart
Carlton Cards	Pier 1 Imports
Circuit City	Radio Shack*
CompUSA	Rent-A-Center
CostPlus	Sephora
Crate & Barrel	Sleepy's
Dick's Sporting Goods	Staples
Duty Free Americas, Inc.	Toys R Us

GameStop	Tractor Supply
GNC (General Nutrition Center)	U.S. Postal Service
Guitar Center	Verizon Wireless
Hancock Fabric	
Transportation	
Amtrak	Metrorail (DC)
Long Island Railroad	NJ Transit
Metro North Railroad (New York)	SEPTA (Pennsylvania)
MTA NYC Transit	

(*Denotes retailers that may not offer the use of PIN-based ATM/debit cards.)

Further information on NYCE, including available ATM machines, U.S. retailers, and participating financial institutions and related fees can be found at www.nyce.net/index.jsp.

Opening a U.S. Bank Account

Consider opening a U.S. bank account for your American banking needs. In most cases, nothing should prevent you from opening a U.S. account. However, because of American and Canadian securities regulations, opening an investment account in the United States in most cases won't be possible for snowbirds.

When you open a U.S. bank account, you need to fill out IRS Form W-8BEN — *Certificate of Foreign Status of Beneficial Owner for United States Tax Withholding* (reproduced below), which needs to be on file with the bank to confirm your non-resident status. (Recall our comments in Chapter 2 on the U.S. tax scam directed at unsuspecting snowbirds related to this form.)

Interest earned within an American bank account is exempt from U.S. taxation, which is the opposite from Americans generating interest in a Canadian bank account, which is subject to a 10% withholding tax. There is a current proposal to eliminate the withholding tax on interest in the next Canada–U.S. Tax Treaty amendments.

Form **W-8BEN**

(Rev. February 2006)

Department of the Treasury
Internal Revenue Service

Certificate of Foreign Status of Beneficial Owner for United States Tax Withholding

▶ Section references are to the Internal Revenue Code. ▶ See separate instructions.
▶ Give this form to the withholding agent or payer. Do not send to the IRS.

OMB No. 1545-1621

Do not use this form for:　　　　　　　　　　　　　　　　　　　　　　　　　　　Instead, use Form
- A U.S. citizen or other U.S. person, including a resident alien individual W-9
- A person claiming that income is effectively connected with the conduct
  of a trade or business in the United States W-8ECI
- A foreign partnership, a foreign simple trust, or a foreign grantor trust (see instructions for exceptions) . . . . . . W-8ECI or W-8IMY
- A foreign government, international organization, foreign central bank of issue, foreign tax-exempt organization,
  foreign private foundation, or government of a U.S. possession that received effectively connected income or that is
  claiming the applicability of section(s) 115(2), 501(c), 892, 895, or 1443(b) (see instructions) . . . . W-8ECI or W-8EXP

Note: *These entities should use Form W-8BEN if they are claiming treaty benefits or are providing the form only to claim they are a foreign person exempt from backup withholding.*

- A person acting as an intermediary W-8IMY

Note: *See instructions for additional exceptions.*

Part I　Identification of Beneficial Owner (See instructions.)

1　Name of individual or organization that is the beneficial owner | 2　Country of incorporation or organization

3　Type of beneficial owner: ☐ Individual ☐ Corporation ☐ Disregarded entity ☐ Partnership ☐ Simple trust
☐ Grantor trust ☐ Complex trust ☐ Estate ☐ Government ☐ International organization
☐ Central bank of issue ☐ Tax-exempt organization ☐ Private foundation

4　Permanent residence address (street, apt. or suite no., or rural route). **Do not use a P.O. box or in-care-of address.**

City or town, state or province. Include postal code where appropriate. | Country (do not abbreviate)

5　Mailing address (if different from above)

City or town, state or province. Include postal code where appropriate. | Country (do not abbreviate)

6　U.S. taxpayer identification number, if required (see instructions) ☐ SSN or ITIN ☐ EIN | 7　Foreign tax identifying number, if any (optional)

8　Reference number(s) (see instructions)

Part II　Claim of Tax Treaty Benefits (if applicable)

9　I certify that (check all that apply):
a ☐ The beneficial owner is a resident of ....within the meaning of the income tax treaty between the United States and that country.
b ☐ If required, the U.S. taxpayer identification number is stated on line 6 (see instructions).
c ☐ The beneficial owner is not an individual, derives the item (or items) of income for which the treaty benefits are claimed, and, if applicable, meets the requirements of the treaty provision dealing with limitation on benefits (see instructions).
d ☐ The beneficial owner is not an individual, is claiming treaty benefits for dividends received from a foreign corporation or interest from a U.S. trade or business of a foreign corporation, and meets qualified resident status (see instructions).
e ☐ The beneficial owner is related to the person obligated to pay the income within the meaning of section 267(b) or 707(b), and will file Form 8833 if the amount subject to withholding received during a calendar year exceeds, in the aggregate, $500,000.

10　**Special rates and conditions** (if applicable—see instructions): The beneficial owner is claiming the provisions of Article .... of the treaty identified on line 9a above to claim a .... % rate of withholding on (specify type of income): ....
Explain the reasons the beneficial owner meets the terms of the treaty article: ....
....

Part III　Notional Principal Contracts

11 ☐ I have provided or will provide a statement that identifies those notional principal contracts from which the income is **not** effectively connected with the conduct of a trade or business in the United States. I agree to update this statement as required.

Part IV　Certification

Under penalties of perjury, I declare that I have examined the information on this form and to the best of my knowledge and belief it is true, correct, and complete. I further certify under penalties of perjury that:
1 I am the beneficial owner (or am authorized to sign for the beneficial owner) of all the income to which this form relates,
2 The beneficial owner is not a U.S. person,
3 The income to which this form relates is (a) not effectively connected with the conduct of a trade or business in the United States, (b) effectively connected but is not subject to tax under an income tax treaty, or (c) the partner's share of a partnership's effectively connected income, **and**
4 For broker transactions or barter exchanges, the beneficial owner is an exempt foreign person as defined in the instructions.
Furthermore, I authorize this form to be provided to any withholding agent that has control, receipt, or custody of the income of which I am the beneficial owner or any withholding agent that can disburse or make payments of the income of which I am the beneficial owner.

Sign Here ▶ _____ | Date (MM-DD-YYYY) | Capacity in which acting
Signature of beneficial owner (or individual authorized to sign for beneficial owner)

For Paperwork Reduction Act Notice, see separate instructions.　Cat. No. 25047Z　Form **W-8BEN** (Rev. 2-2006)

✿ *Printed on Recycled Paper*

In some cases, you may find bankers in the United States providing IRS Form W-9 — *Request for Taxpayer Identification Number and Certification.* This form applies only to American citizens and residents, so you shouldn't complete it. The W8-BEN form is the only IRS form that you need to complete to open a regular personal U.S. bank account.

Any U.S. bank interest earnings are subject to Canadian income tax and need to be reported on your Canadian return.

Here's an example. Tim Hortonowski, a Canadian snowbird and U.S. non-resident, opens an American checking/savings account in the U.S. community that he frequents on an annual basis. Tim completes Form W-8BEN for filing with his American bank. The account earns U.S.$1,250 of interest. No U.S. withholding tax will be imposed on the account in the United States. Tim isn't required to report the U.S. interest on a U.S. tax return. However, he does have to report the interest, adjusted for Canadian dollars, on his Canadian income tax return.

Taxation of U.S. Investments

It's important to understand how U.S. investment income is taxed for American and Canadian income tax purposes. In some cases, a U.S. return must be filed by a snowbird. In other cases, the withholding tax imposed at the source on U.S. investment income will satisfy U.S. tax requirements.

U.S.-Source Interest-Bearing Investments

Certain interest-bearing investments are exempt from U.S. taxation for Canadians. These investments include U.S. treasury bills, federal, state, and municipal bonds, and U.S. corporate bonds issued after July 18, 1984. As mentioned above, bank account interest is also exempt from withholding tax. Interest earned by you on other bonds and debt obligations is generally subject to a U.S. withholding tax of 10%. Any interest earned on a bond or other debt instrument in the United States is taxable in Canada and must be declared on your Canadian tax return. Any U.S. tax withheld is eligible as a foreign tax credit on your Canadian return.

For example, Steve Canuck, a Canadian snowbird and U.S. non-resident, attends a local investment seminar with a snowbird neighbour from the State of New York. At the seminar, the investment advisor touts the merits of a U.S. corporate bond that is currently paying 10% interest on a semi-annual basis. Steve and his friend believe that this is something they should buy to supplement their fixed incomes.

Even though U.S. securities laws restrict Steve from acquiring such a bond in the United States — because of his non-resident status — he uses his American mailing address and his Individual Tax Identification Number (ITIN) that was issued when he sold some U.S. real estate a few years back. They each purchase U.S.$25,000 of this bond. Steve is required to file IRS Form 1040NR and report the U.S.-source income and, under the treaty, remit 10% of this amount with his tax return. He is also required to report the interest, adjusted for Canadian dollars, on his Canadian income tax return. The 10% U.S. tax paid on the U.S.-source income becomes a foreign tax credit on his Canadian return.

Steve should also seek advice from his Canadian financial advisor and tax specialist about the legal and securities compliance issues with respect to holding a U.S. investment account as a resident of Canada.

U.S.-Source Dividends

Dividend income earned in the United States is taxable in Canada. This income needs to be included, once adjusted for Canadian dollars, on your Canadian tax return. The 15% U.S. withholding tax would be eligible as a foreign tax credit on the Canadian tax return. As long as this tax is withheld, you don't have to file a U.S. income tax return. To make sure that you do not expose yourself to double taxation on the income, work with a tax professional knowledgeable in Canada-U.S. taxation matters.

Capital Gains

Capital gains realized on the sale of U.S. shares held in a Canadian investment account are not subject to U.S. capital gains or withholding tax. These gains are taxable in Canada only. In addition, any capital gains generated by the sale of shares or mutual funds located in the United States (if you can find a way to open an account) are generally exempt from taxation in the United States. This exemption is due primarily to the Canada-U.S. Tax Treaty, but you should note that it doesn't apply to U.S. citizens living in Canada.

Here's an example for investment income. Carla, a Canadian snowbird and U.S. non-resident, has an investment account in Canada that holds various U.S. stocks. Most of the commonly held U.S. stocks also pay a dividend. When the dividend is paid, a treaty-mandated 15% of the dividend amount must be withheld at source by the financial institution. Carla doesn't have to file a U.S. income tax return on the U.S.-source dividends, but the Canadian investment firm will issue a Canadian T3 or T5 slip reporting the U.S.-source dividends as well as the tax withheld. Carla needs to report this information on her Canadian income tax return.

Management of Canadian Investment and Retirement Accounts in the United States

Current U.S. securities rules generally don't permit Canadian investment representatives and dealers to make purchases of Canadian securities in non-registered and registered (RRSP or RRIF) accounts unless the specific security, the investment dealer, and the investment representative involved all have the appropriate U.S. securities registration. Such registration has been impractical in most cases.

On June 23, 2000, the U.S. Securities and Exchange Commission (SEC) announced that Canadians living or spending time south of the border will be allowed to actively manage their Registered Retirement Savings Plans (RRSPS) and Registered Retirement Income Funds (RRIFS) when residing in the United States.

Prior to this change, U.S. laws restricted the investment management activities in Canadian accounts for Canadians living or spending time in the United States. The new rules apply only to registered retirement accounts (RRSPS, RRIFS, LIRAS) and not to any other kind of Canadian investment account. It's also important to note that these rules apply only to those states that have adopted the Investment Dealers Association proposals. Currently, 45 states have adopted special registration or exemption from registration for the Canadian firms and their investment representatives when dealing with customers who are snowbirds or permanent residents in the United States. At the time of writing, the five most popular snowbird destination states — Florida, California, Arizona, Hawaii, and Texas — allow for the cross-border retirement trading and management of Canadian registered accounts.

Foreign Exchange Issues

Ask most Canadians, and they can tell you within a penny or two what the Canada-U.S. exchange rate is. In our opinion, some Canadians' national pride rises and falls in relation to the exchange rate of the Canadian dollar to the American dollar. Nowhere have we dealt with more confusion or deliberation over decisions than in the area of currency exchange. It appears that the record high closing rate for the Canadian dollar occurred on August 31, 1957, and again on October 31, 1959, at $1.05485, with the record low closing set on January 18, 2002, at $0.61989.

One of the greatest concerns of most snowbirds is the plight of the Canadian dollar against the U.S. dollar. Rising health care expenses, travel costs, and lifestyle expenditures can take a toll on the fixed Canadian dollar incomes of snowbirds. To the extent that you are committed to a long-term retirement lifestyle in the United States, you should adopt a similar commitment to your investment income and portfolio management approach.

If you are planning on living in the United States for some portion of each year, you will need U.S. dollars to meet those expenses. To provide those American dollars, you should diversify your investment and retirement portfolios to include assets that produce U.S. dollar income. This is an excellent way to hedge your future U.S. dollar requirements. Investments that generate American dollars will allow you to pay for some of your expenses each year without ever having to exchange Canadian dollars.

This section aims to clear up some misconceptions and confusion so you can begin to move forward with confidence in this area.

Myth: You Lose Money When You Convert

One of the biggest misconceptions out there is that you "lose money when you exchange Canadian loonies for U.S. dollars." Nothing could be further from the truth. The thinking goes, if you lose money during currency exchange, there must be ways of making money during it too!

On one day in 2007, the following exchange rates were observed:

$1 Canadian = $0.898 U.S. = $6.99 Hong Kong = $29.36 Taiwan = $91,122 Zimbabwe.

The first thing to notice is that all of these countries use the "dollar" as the name for their currency, and therein lies the problem. Because the currency has the same name, people assume it should have the same value. It does not. This is because they are different currencies, from different countries, with a different value associated with each one. A Polish zloty is different from a U.S. dollar, which is different from the Euro, which is different from an Italian lira, which is different from a Canadian loonie. Different currencies from different countries (even if they have the same name) have different values ascribed to them by the supply and demand of a particular country's currency in the world. Stop thinking about Canadian dollars and start calling them Canadian loonies — doing so will help you to start dealing with the currency exchange issue.

To further illustrate the point, suppose you exchange one Canadian loonie into one U.S. dollar. According to the example above, you will receive U.S.$0.898 for your Canadian loonie. People believe that, since they are getting 10.2¢ less, they have "lost" money. If that argument holds true, then take your Canadian dollar and exchange it into Zimbabwe dollars, and you will "gain" $91,121! If you exchange 100 Canadian dollars, you could become a millionaire in Zimbabwe! But we all know a Zimbabwe millionaire is a lot different from a Canadian millionaire, who is different from an American millionaire. Consider as well that, if you were to convert your U.S.$0.898 right back into Canadian loonies the next day, how much would you receive? You're right, pretty much one Canadian dollar (less any transaction fee), so where did you lose money in the currency exchange? And where did you gain money?

The real issue is the difference in living expenses you will incur in the United States versus Canada. If the expenses (food, shelter, taxes, gas, autos, health care, etc.) are lower in the United States and your currency conversion leaves you with fewer "dollars" in your pocket, then the currency exchange may be inconsequential because you have lower living expenses in the United States for the same lifestyle. We all know it is cheaper to live in Zimbabwe, but we have to look at other aspects of the lifestyle there to get some insights into whether becoming a millionaire in Zimbabwe is worthwhile.

The other factor that comes into play is the fluctuation in exchange rates over time. For example, if you have a fixed Canadian pension, you could face a loss of purchasing power in the

United States if the Canada-U.S. exchange rate declines, particularly if your Canadian pension is your primary source of income.

Myth: Someone Knows Where the Exchange Rate Is Going

We can't tell you how many times people have asked for our opinion on where the Canada-U.S. exchange rate is going. The resounding answer is "We have no idea," but in our view "a bird in the hand is better than 1.01 birds in the bush." First, as seen in the graph below, waiting for a better exchange rate has been the wrong thing to do for the majority of the past 36 years, until of late. Second, in 1971, who knew that this would be the case? Investment research has shown that even the most prudent currency traders, economists, and investment managers can't make successful predictions over any extended period of time. If they could, they wouldn't tell you, and they would no longer need to make predictions — they'd have more money than they had ever dreamed of getting.

A number of factors influence Canada-U.S. exchange rates and make it impossible to predict where the rate is going over the long term with any consistency. The causes of currency

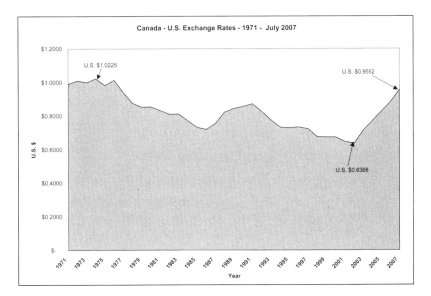

exchange fluctuations are what economists love to talk about at parties. We have limited knowledge in this area and offer you the following key factors that the experts agree influence the Canada-U.S. exchange rate:

- the difference in inflation rates between Canada and the United States;
- the difference in productivity performance;
- the tax system and the tax burden imposed on the citizens of each country;
- the difference in interest rates;
- the difference in non-energy commodity prices;
- the difference in trade and current account balances;
- the difference in fiscal balances;
- the economic growth prospects of each country;
- the political issues and political stability in each country; and
- the need to borrow money by each government.

Despite all of this economist jargon, the bottom line is, whichever currency is more desired by the world, that currency will enjoy a higher exchange rate. It is simple supply and demand, and unfortunately for snowbirds the world wants U.S. dollars more than it wants Canadian dollars at this time (although that has been changing lately with the demand for Canadian oil). Canadian economists have often theorized about how to fix the problem, including abandoning the floating currency and adopting the U.S. currency wholesale, "pegging" the Canadian dollar to the U.S. dollar, or forming a North American "dollar" with the United States and Mexico. We will leave all of this to the economists, but the question to ask is "What do we do now?"

Even though we don't know where the currency rate is going, we do know the Canada-U.S. exchange rate fluctuates about 100 basis points every day. If you need to exchange currency at some point in the future, be aware that there are some currency exchange tools available that you can use to take advantage of the normal fluctuations in the exchange rate. For example, if you need to make a purchase in the short term but want to buy the item at the lower end of the daily fluctuation, you can make a "currency bid" with your currency broker. This is an agreement to purchase a certain amount of foreign currency at a fixed price sometime in the future. This approach allows you to avoid the current spot rate and make a bid to purchase the currency at the lower end of the daily fluctuation. The problem is, if the currency exchange is in an upward pattern, your bid may never get filled. A currency bid can be put out for a maximum of 30 days and canceled or amended at any time with no penalty. Another tool available is a forward contract — an agreement to purchase a certain amount of foreign currency at some point in the future at a rate set today. This is for those who know they will need foreign currency in the future to fund a purchase and want to lock in the exchange rate now. A forward contract can be set for up to a year in advance. The drawback is there's an expense in the currency rate you receive the further out you want the contract to go.

The bottom line is that nobody can predict the future, and really our emotions are driving our decisions . . . and this spells trouble. For example, when we ask "What rate does the exchange rate have to be for you to convert?" we typically get an off-the-cuff answer. Sure enough, when that exchange rate arrives, the decision to wait for an even better rate is made, and the tendency is to ride the exchange rate back down again. Soon your life revolves around the currency exchange section of the newspaper, and your mood for the day is dictated by what happened in currency exchange markets overnight. Is this any way to live? What a way to spend your snowbirding years . . . glued to the newspaper watching the exchange rates (or the stock market, for that matter).

Myth: Wait to Convert

Often people struggle with deciding when to convert their Canadian loonies into American dollars, and "waiting for a better exchange rate" is the game they decide to play. The typical thinking is you can do better if you wait. What many don't realize is they have just made a prediction: the exchange rate will improve by the time they need to exchange loonies into dollars. You have now entered the realm of currency speculation, and frankly there are better ways of speculating on the currency exchange direction, such as buying currency futures contracts. Besides, there are currency traders with millions of dollars and all kinds of equipment monitoring global currency markets in the hope of conducting currency transactions to pay their bills. If there is money to be made in currency speculation, likely many others will make it ahead of you. So how do you determine when to convert your money?

The decision should be made according to what you are trying to achieve (your personal goals). If you want to spend time in the United States on an annual basis, you will have an ongoing need for U.S. dollars, and it may make sense to convert your money now because you know with certainty what the exchange rate is today and how much you'll end up with. Since the Canada-U.S. exchange rate has been on a meteoric rise over the past year, why not exchange a large amount now, avoid any currency speculation, and get on with your life? At a minimum, understand the sensitivity of your financial situation to currency exchange fluctuations and make an informed decision. A prudent, deliberate, ongoing strategy of currency exchanges over a period of time may make the most sense in your situation. Your financial plan should ground your decision making because, without it, important decisions such as exchanging your loonies are driven by emotions, not sound financial reasons. The time to exchange your assets is when you can achieve your desired lifestyle per your financial plan. This approach allows you to remove the currency fluctuations from your retirement projections. This analysis should be one of the criteria you are looking for in your Canada-U.S. financial planner and whether he or she can assist you with this important decision.

Exchanging your Canadian loonies for U.S. dollars can be a very emotional experience, but our firm can provide assistance in this area and help you to make the decision that is right for you. It is worth noting that you want to avoid currency exchange whenever possible because you have to pay the currency exchange broker or bank (see below).

How to Calculate Exchange Rates

Another misconception we often run into is confusion over the calculation of exchange rates. Typically, when c$1 = U.S.$0.85, folks think that c$1.15 = U.S.$1, which is simply not the case. To convert Canadian dollars into American dollars, do the following calculation:

$$\frac{C\$1}{\text{U.S. exchange rate}}$$

If the U.S. exchange rate on a particular day is U.S.$0.8741, what is that in Canadian dollars?

$$C\$1.14 \text{ or } \frac{C\$1}{\text{U.S.}\$0.8741}$$

To convert American dollars into Canadian dollars, do the following calculation:

$$\frac{\text{U.S.}\$1}{\text{Canadian exchange rate}}$$

If the Canadian exchange rate on a particular day is c$1.3424, what is that in American dollars?

$$\text{U.S.}\$0.7449 \text{ or } \frac{\text{U.S.}\$1}{C\$1.3424}$$

To make it easier on yourself, take the price of an item and divide it by the appropriate exchange rate to determine how much it will cost in your desired currency. For example,

- a hat at the outlet mall in Anthem, Arizona, costs U.S.$11: 11/0.85 = C$12.94, while
- a toque at West Edmonton Mall costs C$11: 11/1.176 = U.S.$9.35.

Fact: There Is an Expense to Converting

Although, as we previously discussed, you don't lose money when you "convert" Canadian loonies into U.S. dollars, be aware that there is a transaction expense. Financial institutions "shade" the "spot" rate of the Canada-U.S. exchange rate and use it as another source of profit for shareholders. The way you can tell is to compare the exchange rate online or in the newspaper (the spot rate in the market) with that posted at your local bank or at the "currency exchange carts" at the airport. The difference can be significant. In some cases, using your Canadian credit card in the United States for purchases in U.S. dollars may be better or worse. By shading the exchange rate on your purchases in the United States or applying additional fees, the credit card companies make a small fortune, and you may have no idea. The next time you get your credit card statement look for any additional fees or the rate at which the company exchanged your purchase, and then locate the historical rate — you may grimace. Try to be informed beforehand.

Strategies to Exchange Canadian Dollars for American Dollars

Here are some things you can do to reduce the expense of converting your Canadian loonies into U.S. dollars.

- Ask your currency exchange provider to give you a rate as close to the current spot rate as possible (don't deny the employees from making a living, but make sure you aren't getting gouged). The spot rate is what the market is paying at that moment when the currency exchange is not shaded at all.
- Accumulate your loonies together and convert them into one

lump sum rather than make several smaller transactions because bigger transactions generally get a better exchange rate.

- Determine the expenses associated with using your Canadian dollar credit card for American dollar purchases, and if prohibitive avoid using your Canadian dollar credit card; find a credit card company that issues U.S. dollar cards instead so you can control the exchange rate better rather than take the prevailing rate the credit card company decides for that day.
- Avoid using your bank unless you have a good relationship with it; then ask your banker to give you the spot rate or a rate as close to it as possible.
- Avoid the currency exchange carts in airports or be sure to compare their rates to a discount currency broker or the spot rate in the newspaper or online whenever possible.
- Avoid converting cash since doing so is more expensive. Consider traveler's checks, bank drafts, money orders, or personal checks instead.
- Make sure you do comparative shopping, particularly if you are exchanging large sums.
- If you have an account at a Canadian brokerage firm, it may offer you competitive exchange rates as part of its customer service to you, particularly if you already have a U.S. dollar account.
- American casinos typically provide excellent exchange rates in the hope you'll leave some of your money in their machines or at their tables.
- Unless you go to the casinos, don't typically wait until you get to the United States. Most U.S. banks will not convert your Canadian loonies.
- Leave sufficient U.S. dollars in the United States to meet your currency needs each year or, as mentioned above, enough Canadian dollars in Canada to meet your needs there.

(Thanks to the discount currency broker Custom House Currency, private client team, for their contributions to this section.)

Additional Tips

- Check the condition of your bank debit and credit cards and make sure that the magnetic strips work. If they are "fussy," obtain new or replacement cards before heading south.
- When using ATMs, check for signs of tampering on the machines and card readers. Also check for hidden cameras or people looking over your shoulder when entering your PIN. Shield your fingers on the keypad.
- Don't use unbranded or suspicious-looking ATMs. Convenience stores, shopping malls, and public locations outside banks are typically where you'll find these ATMs. Not only is there a cost for using them, but also there could be a greater chance for "skimming" crimes to occur.
- Don't let cashiers or others enter your PIN for you.
- Make sure you have access to either Internet banking or automatic debiting for any bills that will need to be paid while you are away.
- Let your bank and/or credit card company know that you will be out of the country so that it doesn't cut off access to your card because of abnormal and out-of-country usage.
- Don't use debit cards for large purchases; to preserve your maximum consumer protection, it's better to use a credit card.
- Check bank and credit card statements regularly.
- Make sure your investment or financial advisor is aware of when you will be in the United States. Ensure that your advisor is properly licensed to manage your registered assets while you are there.
- Ensure that your non-registered investment portfolio is properly managed in line with your objectives while you are in the United States.

5

Till Death Do Us Part

U.S. Estate Planning Issues for Snowbirds

The purpose of estate planning is to ensure that your wealth and property are transferred smoothly, with a minimum of depletion to your heirs. One of the most misunderstood and confusing areas for snowbirds is U.S. estate tax. Ignorance of this tax and not undertaking the requisite planning can have serious implications for you and your family not only during your lifetime but at your death as well. Working with a knowledgeable financial advisor familiar with Canada-U.S. estate planning issues can help you plan to eliminate, reduce, or defer this tax. Doing so will also go a long way toward ensuring the transfer of your U.S. wealth to your heirs in as tax and time efficient a manner as possible.

Canada and the United States impose very different systems of tax at death. The Canadian version is effectively a capital gains tax, while the American version is based on the fair market value of all assets owned or considered owned at death.

For Canadian purposes, a Canadian resident is deemed to have disposed of all property at fair market value on the date of death. This forced recognition on death results in a tax on the accrued capital gains on most types of property within your estate. Registered assets such as RRSPS and RIFFS are deemed to be fully distributed at the same time and are taxed as ordinary income in Canada. For married or common law couples in Canada, any tax at the first death may be deferred until the death of the surviving spouse.

For American purposes, U.S. federal estate tax is imposed on the value of assets at the date of death held by citizens and residents of the United States. What is often a surprise to many Canadians and snowbirds is that U.S. estate tax can also be imposed on the value of assets that you hold in the United States or that are considered located there.

In the case of a snowbird who is not a resident or citizen of the United States at the time of death, the amount of your American "taxable estate" is based only on the assets located ("situs") there. Situs is Latin for "location." Under the U.S. Internal Revenue Code, it also means that the asset is "within" the United States. For U.S. estate tax purposes, it represents where the property is deemed to be situated at death. The issue of situs is extremely important because only American situs property is subject to U.S. estate and gift taxes.

American assets that are subject to U.S. estate tax include
- real estate held personally and located in the United States, including vacation properties;
- certain tangible personal property located in the United States (jewelry, art, furnishings, fixtures, boats, and vehicles);
- shares of U.S. corporations, regardless of the location of the share certificates and regardless of where the shares are traded, including those within your RRSP or RIFF;
- debts of American persons, including the U.S. government

(with certain exceptions);
- money market accounts with U.S. brokerage firms;
- cash in a U.S. safe deposit box;
- interests in partnerships carrying on business in the United States;
- golf club memberships (if equity interest); and
- American-based retirement plans, such as IRAS and 401(k) and 403(b) plans.

Assets that are not subject to U.S. estate tax include

- shares of a non-U.S. corporation (regardless of where the corporation's assets are situated);
- American bank deposits;
- certain U.S. corporate bonds that are publicly traded outside the United States;
- certain debt obligations that qualify for the "portfolio debt" exemption from U.S. tax;
- life insurance proceeds payable on a non-resident alien's death; and
- American Depository Receipts (ADR).

We are often asked, "Are ADRs considered a U.S. situs asset?" As indicated above, they are not. An ADR is typically how the stocks of most foreign companies trade on the American stock exchanges. But despite this trading, they are not U.S. situs. The IRS has come out with a couple of revenue rulings that confirm this. The same is true for a Canadian company that trades on an American stock exchange. For example, Nortel Networks trades on the New York Stock Exchange. However, because the company is domiciled in Canada, its shares are not considered U.S. situs.

The most common types of assets subject to U.S. estate tax include American stocks and real estate held personally. The U.S. stocks don't need to be held with an American financial institution to be considered U.S. situs for estate tax purposes. If they are held in your investment portfolio or managed broker-age account in Canada, those shares are considered U.S. situs for estate tax purposes.

One of the most common questions we are asked by Canadian investment advisors, financial planners, and others is "How does the IRS know whether you own U.S. stocks or not?" In most cases, the compliance officers of most Canadian financial institutions and investment dealers are aware of the American estate tax issues imposed on those who die holding U.S. shares personally. When shares are ultimately transferred as part of the estate distribution or probate process, they go through a U.S. transfer agent that generally requires a U.S. estate clearance certificate prior to releasing any proceeds on behalf of the Canadian decedent's estate to beneficiaries.

The Previous U.S. Non-Resident Estate Tax Environment

Prior to 1988, the estates of non-residents of the United States were subject to more favorable rates than those for the estates of citizens and residents of the United States. Previous to these changes, non-residents of the United States were subject to the same levels of estate tax that applied to U.S. citizens and residents.

In November 1996, the Third Protocol of the Canada-U.S. Income Tax Convention (or Treaty) was changed to provide a greater level of relief for Canadians who held U.S. property at death. Without the relief provided by the treaty changes, many Canadians were subject to very onerous U.S. estate taxes in addition to the Canadian capital gains tax at death. This "double taxation" predicament was addressed in a new article — Article XXIX B — of the treaty with respect to deaths after November 10, 1996.

Generally, the new article increased the unified credit available to the estates of Canadians, provided for foreign tax credits in Canada and the United States for death taxes paid to the other jurisdiction, and expanded the circumstances in which both countries offered tax relief where property is left to a spouse or a qualifying trust. The article also provided some degree of relief with respect to charitable gifts made at death. A summary of the new treaty provisions that can benefit you follows.

The New Prorated Unified Credit

Pursuant to the updated treaty, you are now entitled — on a prorated basis — for the full unified credit. The unified credit is a direct dollar-for-dollar offset against any U.S. federal estate taxes owing. Prior to this change, you were entitled to an exemption of only U.S.$60,000 for American estate tax purposes. Under the new rules, the credit can now be somewhere between U.S.$13,000 and $780,800 (for the 2007 and 2008 tax years), but it depends on the proportion of your total assets situated in the United States.

In terms of planning guidelines, if your worldwide gross estate (adjusted for U.S. dollars) is less than U.S.$2 million, American estate tax would now be offset through the available unified credit provided for under the treaty. Furthermore, if you are married and your worldwide estate doesn't exceed approximately U.S.$4 million at the time of your death, and your American situs assets pass to your Canadian surviving spouse, no U.S. federal estate tax will be imposed at your death. The prorated unified credit is calculated as follows:

$$\frac{\text{applicable exclusion amount x value of your assets situated in the U.S.}}{\text{value of your worldwide gross estate}}$$

Bear in mind that the value of your worldwide estate will include assets not normally taxed or provided for under Canadian tax law. These assets include the value of your Canadian RRSPs and RIFFs, life insurance proceeds you are considered to "own" under American rules, and the value of your Canadian business and/or personal residence. Furthermore, as part of the calculation of your worldwide estate, if you were receiving a corporate pension plan distribution that would continue in full or on a reduced basis to your surviving spouse, the present value of the future payments to your surviving spouse must also be included in your worldwide estate. In fact, the calculated pro-rated unified credit will be permitted only to the extent that full disclosure of your worldwide assets is provided to the IRS. Moreover, every filed IRS Form 706NA — *Estate Tax Return for Nonresidents of the U.S.* is reviewed manually by the IRS, and approximately 60% are chosen for further examination. This process generally focuses on the correct valuation of assets and on determining the existence of unreported U.S. situs assets. Not only do you have to fully disclose and support assets that have nothing to do with the United States, but you also have to include a copy of your will and other relevant documents. It's important to note that the IRS examiners who review and assess Form 706NA are generally "the cream of the crop" and focus almost exclusively on this area of taxation. This specialization makes it rather difficult to "pull the wool toque over their eyes" (not that you would ever consider doing this).

Small U.S. Estates

Under Article XXIX B(8) of the treaty, an exemption from U.S. estate tax is provided to you if the entire value of your world-wide estate is less than U.S.$1.2 million — with recent American tax changes now U.S.$2 million. However, this special treaty exemption doesn't apply to U.S. real estate or personal property forming part of the business property of an American perma-nent establishment or fixed base.

Therefore, if your worldwide estate (adjusted for U.S. dol-lars) doesn't exceed U.S.$2 million, and doesn't include American real or business property yet includes American shares (which are included in the value up to the U.S.$2 million threshold), no U.S. estate tax exposure would exist at your death. However, if your worldwide estate (adjusted for U.S. dol-lars) is one American dollar over the U.S.$2 million threshold, estate tax would need to be calculated, and an American estate tax exposure may exist. However, as previously discussed, if you are married and your Canadian surviving spouse were to receive your American assets, so long as your worldwide estate doesn't exceed U.S.$4 million, no U.S. estate tax would exist.

Marital Tax Credit

In addition to the prorated unified credit provided under the updated treaty, Articles XXIX B(3) and (4) provide a marital credit against U.S. estate tax on property passing to your surviving spouse where you and your spouse meet certain requirements. The benefit of this treaty election is that it effectively allows you to "double up" on the prorated unified credit at the first death.

The requirements that must be met to take the marital tax credit are

- the decedent at the time of death must have been a citizen of the United States or a resident of either Canada or the United States;
- at the time of the decedent's death, the surviving spouse must have been a resident of either Canada or the United States;
- if, at the time of the decedent's death, both the decedent and the surviving spouse were resident in the United States, one or both of them must have been a Canadian citizen; and
- the executor(s) of the decedent's estate must elect to take the benefits (marital credit) provided for under Article XXIX B(3) and waive irrevocably the benefits of any estate tax marital deduction that would have been allowed under the U.S. domestic law.

The credit provided for in Article XXIX B(4) is calculated as

- the unified credit available to the estate (without regard to any credit allowed previously with respect to any gift made by the individual) and

- the amount of estate tax that would otherwise be imposed by the United States on the transfer of qualifying property.

The amount of the marital credit can't exceed the initial pro-rated unified credit; therefore, the credit will be of little use where only a small portion of your worldwide assets are located in the United States at the time of death. For larger estates, a choice has to be made between tax deferral offered through a qualified domestic trust (QDOT, discussed later in this chapter) that would qualify as a "spousal trust" under the Canadian Income Tax Act as opposed to having your spouse directly inherit the American property outside of using a QDOT.

The effect of this new provision can be significant and may fully eliminate any U.S. estate tax exposure upon the first death. An example of how this provision can apply at death is presented later in the chapter.

Canadian Foreign Tax Credits for U.S. Estate Tax

This is one of the most welcome changes within the updated treaty. Article XXIX B(6) now provides that any U.S. federal estate and state inheritance tax is allowed as a credit against any income tax imposed in Canada for the taxation year in which you died. On the surface, it appears that your estate may be eligible to benefit from these credits, but the credit for U.S. estate tax payable could be limited or unavailable if

- you had little or no U.S.-source income in the year (no accrued or unrealized capital gains on American assets), or
- there is other U.S.-source income (other than the accrued American gains) but little or no Canadian tax payable on the income because of the credit used for U.S. income taxes paid.

Relative to specific wording in Article XXIX B(6), gains related to U.S. shares may not be deemed to arise in the United States for the purposes of the provisions of the article. The credit won't be provided for in circumstances where taxes payable were the result of a deferral or rollover in Canada to a spouse or spousal trust. Therefore, it is critical to work with a qualified Canada-U.S. advisor to make optimal use of foreign tax credits in Canada for U.S. estate taxes paid.

The Current and Future U.S. Non-Resident Estate Tax Environment

Due to significant American tax law changes passed in June 2001, the former top U.S. estate tax rate of 55% has decreased and will continue to decrease from 2000 to 2009. The maximum estate tax rate for 2007 is 45% for estates greater than U.S.$1.5 million. In 2010, the American estate tax is scheduled to be repealed. However, after 2010, without further legislative changes, the former U.S. estate tax rate (maximum rate of 55%) and exemption environment (U.S.$1 million) will be brought back for the tax year 2011 and beyond.

As of June 8, 2006, the Senate voted to fully repeal the U.S. estate tax. However, the vote was defeated by a close margin, keeping the estate tax alive in the United States for the foreseeable future. With the House and Senate now controlled by the Democrats, the prospects of a full repeal of the U.S. estate tax are less likely. However, there are still some American politicians who hope to develop some level of compromise for the U.S. estate tax. Some proposals suggest increasing the amount of assets exempt from U.S. estate tax to as high as U.S.$5 million, with a maximum estate tax of 15% — to be in line with the long-term capital gains rate in the United States. Still others believe it should be left alone or even return to the exemption and tax levels prior to the changes of 2001 (as scheduled). This much we know: Congress will continue tinkering with the U.S. estate tax system, and change will be the only constant.

With the new tax treaty provision computations, the ever-changing value of your worldwide estate, the determination of jointly held asset values (discussed later in the chapter), and the scheduled U.S. estate tax changes and future legislative uncertainty, if you personally own American assets it's important that you keep abreast of the U.S. estate tax environment and its impact on your estate plans.

The tables below list the present marginal U.S. estate and gift tax rates as well as future exclusion amounts and maximum tax rates.

Table 5.1
U.S. Federal Estate and Gift Taxes (Unified Transfer Tax Rate Schedule) — Tax Year 2007*

If the taxable estate is ...		then ...		
over	but not over	tentative tax is is (A)	plus (B)	of excess over (C)
$0	$10,000	$0	18%	$0
10,000	20,000	1,800	20%	10,000
20,000	40,000	3,800	22%	20,000
40,000	60,000	8,200	24%	40,000
60,000	80,000	13,000	26%	60,000
80,000	100,000	18,200	28%	80,000
100,000	150,000	23,800	30%	100,000
150,000	250,000	38,800	32%	150,000
250,000	500,000	70,800	34%	250,000
500,000	750,000	155,800	37%	500,000
750,000	1,000,000	248,300	39%	750,000
1,000,000	1,250,000	345,800	41%	1,000,000
1,250,000	1,500,000	448,300	43%	1,250,000
1,500,000	and over	555,800	45%	1,500,000

*From 2007, the maximum rate will remain at 45% from that point on until the estate tax is repealed in 2010.

Each person has a unified credit (a "coupon") that reduces the amount of estate or gift taxes that must be paid. For 2007, this credit is $780,800 or the equivalent of having $2 million of assets not subject to federal estate tax. In 2009, the unified credit will increase, as will the equivalent amount of estate assets that can be passed without any estate tax (the "applicable exclusion amount"). The table below shows these changes.

Table 5.2
U.S. Unified Credit and Applicable Exclusion Amount after Economic Growth and Tax Relief Reconciliation Act of 2001

Year	Unified Credit	Applicable Exclusion Amount	Maximum Tax Rate
2007	$780,800	$2,000,000	45%
2008	780,800	2,000,000	45%
2009	1,455,800	3,500,000	45%
2010	Estate tax repealed	Estate tax repealed	Estate tax repealed
2011 and later	345,800	1,000,000	55%

Calculating Your U.S. Non-Resident Estate Tax
Determine the Value of Your Worldwide Estate

For U.S. estate tax purposes, your worldwide estate includes the fair market value of all assets at death, including RRSPs, RRIFs, Canadian investment accounts, your principal residence, and any other real estate and business interests in Canada and all the necessary documentation to back up these numbers. In some cases, the value of life insurance proceeds owned at death forms part of the worldwide estate for American estate tax purposes as well. That is why estate tax returns are rarely sent to the IRS in an envelope; they are usually in a box!

As a general guideline, and assuming that there have been no prior U.S. taxable gifts, the following U.S. dollar estate threshold amounts should be kept in mind.

- If your American-situated assets are worth less than U.S.$60,000 at death, no U.S. estate tax exposure exists regardless of the value of your worldwide estate.
- If your worldwide estate is less than U.S.$2 million at death, there is no exposure on any American- situated assets.
- If your worldwide estate is worth more than U.S.$2 million, U.S. estate tax exposure could exist on all American-situated assets.

The "taxable estate" for estate tax purposes is the gross value of all your property situated in the United States less allowable deductions. The most significant deductions are

- amounts left to your spouse if the spouse is an American citizen (and therefore subject to U.S. estate tax upon death);
- amounts transferred to a qualified domestic trust (QDOT);
- a deduction for a share of your liabilities at the time of death that the estate becomes liable for, including Canadian income taxes payable; and
- a deduction for a *non-recourse* mortgage encumbering U.S. property (discussed later in the chapter).

Example of U.S. Estate Tax Exposure — Single Person

- Gord is a single person who snowbirds regularly in Arizona for three months.
- He passes away unexpectedly in July 2007.
- His financial information is as follows.
    - o His worldwide estate (assets in Canada and the United States) is U.S.$5 million.
    - o His condo in Arizona is worth U.S.$500,000.
    - o The condo was used personally.

Calculating Gord's U.S. estate tax is a five-step process.

Step 1: Determine the Value of Gord's Worldwide Estate

Gord's worldwide estate includes all assets owned in Canada, including his Canadian residence, registered assets, investment accounts, and business interests, and it may include any life insurance proceeds upon his death. As presented above, his worldwide estate adjusted for U.S. dollars is $5 million, and his Arizona condo is worth $500,000.

Going through our rule of thumb outlined above, because his worldwide estate is greater than $2 million, Gord is subject to U.S. estate tax on the Arizona property. Bear in mind that, if Gord also held American shares in his Canadian investment or registered accounts, these assets would be included in his U.S. taxable estate.

Step 2: Determine the Estate Tax Imposed on U.S. Assets

Using Table 5.1, let's calculate the amount of U.S. estate tax payable on the value of Gord's American situs assets. In his case, if you look at Table 5.1, his U.S. estate tax is calculated as follows:

U.S. estate tax: C x B + A (excess over amount [column C] x estate tax rate [column B] + tentative tax [column A])
= **$155,800** ($500,000 – $250,000 x 34% + $70,800)

Step 3: Determine the Estate Tax Credit (Exemption)

As discussed above, snowbirds are entitled to an exemption from U.S. estate tax. This credit is available only on a prorata basis and is determined by dividing your American situs assets into your U.S. dollar worldwide estate. The percentage result is then multiplied against the exemption available in the year of death (an exemption that will change, as noted, from 2007 to 2010). The credit is calculated as follows:

$$\frac{\text{Applicable exemption amount X Value of U.S. situs assets}}{\text{Value of decedent's worldwide gross estate}}$$

Step 4: Multiply the Result from Step 3 against the Exemption Available in the Year of Death

Based on the U.S. tax law changes of 2001, the applicable exclusion amounts (exemption amounts) will be changing from 2007 through 2010. Therefore, the prorated credit amount determined in step 3 must be multiplied against the exemption available in the year of death to determine how much of an estate tax credit can be applied against the estate tax. Gord's estate tax credit would be $78,080.

$780,800 (from step 2) x (10% (from step 3) = $78,080

Step 5: Determine Additional Credits against U.S. Estate Tax

In Gord's case, the available unified credit calculated in step 4 is subtracted from the result in step 2 (his U.S. estate tax) to find his total U.S. estate tax payable.

$155,800 − $78,080 (from step 4) = $77,720

Example of U.S. Estate Tax Exposure — Married Couple

If Gord was married to Donna, also a Canadian, but the other details of his estate were the same as presented above, his estate could be entitled to the additional marital credit provided for in Articles xxix b(3) and (4) of the treaty. This effectively allows his estate to use the credit twice ("double up") at his death. In his case, the unified credit calculated in step 4 above can be used as a marital credit as well.

The "married" Gord U.S. estate tax result is calculated as follows:

Net U.S. estate tax: (U.S. estate tax from step 2 — available unified credit from step 4 — marital credit available) = **$0 ($155,800 − $78,080 − $78,080)**

In our examples, the net U.S. estate tax imposed on his Arizona condominium would be reduced from $77,720 (single) to $0 (married).

Strategies to Reduce, Defer, or Eliminate U.S. Non-Resident Estate Tax

An expression we often use in our firm is "We do not want to complicate your life anymore than it already is." Unfortunately, many professionals who end up working with clients who require U.S. non-resident estate planning do complicate their lives. Rather than taking a step back and first quantifying the level of U.S. estate tax exposure that a client might face, they are quick to recommend a strategy that, at the end of the day, may not be appropriate for that client. The costs versus the benefits of many of the strategies we see implemented in many cases just don't make sense. They likely make greater sense to the advisors, for they are the ones getting paid for complicating the lives of the unwary (see Chapter 7 on how to select an advisor).

We have seen situations where application of the updated treaty changes immediately solved the problems for our clients. Furthermore, in some cases, simple gifting or the retitling of property ownership would have been far more effective than the establishment of a sophisticated structure to hold property or U.S. shares. We have seen clients implementing elaborate structures to hold their U.S. real estate for investment purposes and having to pay U.S. tax of 39% versus the much lower personal long-term capital gains rate of 15% upon the sale of the property. Yes, such structures could have solved the estate tax problem upon the death of the shareholder, but given the objectives of the clients and the costs of setting up some of these structures (U.S.$10,000 or more plus future annual administrative costs) other more tax- and cost-efficient alternatives were available.

The recent tax treaty changes require you to first "run the numbers" to determine the level of exposure you might have. After that, you need to ask yourself the following types of questions.

- Are you single or married?
- What is the value of the U.S. property you hold?
- How old are you? How is your health? What is your life expectancy?

- Will any family members be involved in owning or using the U.S. property?
- Do you want to keep the property in the family? What do your heirs want?
- Are your family members competent? Does everyone get along? How old are your family members?
- Will you be using the U.S. property personally? Will you rent it out?
- What kind of annual expenses (property taxes, utilities, and other costs) are involved with maintaining the property?
- Will the property have a mortgage?
- How long do you anticipate holding the property? Will it be held after the death of the first owner?
- What is the value of your worldwide estate in U.S. dollars?
- What is the value of other American situs assets that you hold, such as U.S. shares?
- Are you contemplating moving permanently to the United States?
- Would the income tax at death in Canada be sufficient as a foreign tax credit against any U.S. estate tax?

With these questions in mind, the following strategies should be undertaken only with the help of competent professionals who are knowledgeable in Canada-U.S. tax and estate planning matters. These strategies can reduce your U.S. estate tax exposure while minimizing or eliminating the U.S. gift tax. Other strategies could be used to coordinate foreign tax credits in order to minimize tax payable at death in Canada and the United States. The following strategies are applicable to non-residents and non-citizens of the United States; American residents and citizens cannot avail themselves of these strategies. (If you require additional information related to U.S. estate tax planning for American citizens or residents, consult our companion books *The Canadian in America* and *The American in Canada*.)

Sell U.S. Shares in Your Canadian Investment Accounts

One of the simplest things you can do to reduce or eliminate your U.S. estate tax is to sell the American shares you own now and avoid purchasing any in the future. If you don't personally own American shares at death, there can be no U.S. estate tax because there are no American-situated assets. However, before you sell everything, be sure to calculate the estate tax savings against the capital gains taxes you would pay in Canada on any accrued gains. If these gains are substantial, it may make sense to pay the U.S. estate tax and use foreign tax credits under the tax treaty to create some level of relief through the matching of foreign tax credits upon filing American estate tax and Canadian income tax returns.

One question your investment manager may have is "How are we going to get exposure to the U.S. market?" There are exchange-traded funds listed on the Toronto Stock Exchange that hold the S&P 500 (500 largest companies in the United States) that are very inexpensive to own. Because these funds are registered and listed in Canada, they aren't considered U.S. situs.

Gift U.S. Property Prior to Death

Property gifted prior to your death is not subject to U.S. estate tax. However, the United States has a separate gift tax imposed on the gifting of tangible American-situated assets (i.e., U.S. real estate). The reason for the gift tax is to prevent people from giving their entire estates away on their deathbeds to avoid paying estate taxes. Intangible property includes assets such as U.S. shares or U.S. debts. Note that intangible American property is not subject to gift tax by non-residents of the United States.

Under American law, the IRS provides an annual exemption from gift tax on gifts of tangible property made during one's lifetime. For tax year 2007, the annual gift exemption amount is U.S.$12,000. There is no limit to the number of recipients for which an individual may claim this annual exemption. The annual limit for gifts to a non-U.S.-citizen spouse in 2007 is U.S.$125,000.

Most Canadians are completely unaware of the rules surrounding gifting in the United States. In Canada, Canadians can gift cash or assets to spouses, children, or others with no gift tax repercussions because that form of tax doesn't exist in Canada. There are other Canadian tax rules, such as the income tax "attribution rules," when gifting to spouses or children in lower tax brackets and the deemed disposition when gifting to a trust.

If you are considering gifting U.S. assets prior to death to avoid the inclusion of such assets in your U.S. gross estate, you need to consider the Canadian income tax implications of this strategy as well. For example, a gift of appreciated American shares to a son or daughter would trigger capital gains tax for Canadian tax purposes. The income tax attribution laws in Canada also apply if the recipient of the gift is a child under the age of 18.

Ensure Your U.S. Worldwide Estate Is below U.S.$2 Million

Reducing your worldwide estate to below the U.S.$2 million (single) or U.S.$4 million (married) threshold ensures that any American situs assets held personally won't be subject to U.S. estate taxes. Keep in mind that this doesn't apply to American real estate or business interests.

Hold U.S. Shares in Canadian Mutual Funds

As mentioned earlier, Canadian mutual funds and exchange-traded funds that hold U.S. stocks aren't considered as American situs assets because of their domestic corporate or trust structure. Therefore, any U.S. shares acquired or held within a Canadian mutual fund that invests in American securities won't be subject to U.S. estate tax upon your death. Recent publicity has shown that Canada has some of the highest mutual fund expenses in the world, and the higher the expenses the lower your return. We encourage you to be selective and scrutinize the expenses associated with Canadian mutual funds holding U.S. stocks.

Hold U.S. Shares through a Canadian Corporation

Holding U.S. shares through a Canadian corporation rather than personally exempts them from U.S. estate tax. At your death, the corporation doesn't end. Making use of a Canadian corporation effectively changes the location of the U.S. shares to Canada. While this is often a viable solution for avoiding or reducing U.S. estate tax, it does require proper structuring of the corporation.

- Under Section 85.1.1 of the Canadian Income Tax Act, shares may be transferred to a Canadian corporation on a tax-deferred basis.
- Beyond the initial setup costs of the corporation, there are ongoing costs to maintain it, such as additional legal and accounting fees, so be sure you take them into account in your overall rate of return.
- Appropriate corporate formalities must be observed.
- Any investment income earned by the corporation on its U.S. shares (dividends, interest) is subject to double tax — once when earned and again when paid out in the form of dividends. These combined taxes may be higher than the tax the individual would pay if the assets were held directly.

Use Life Insurance to Cover the Taxes at Death

If you want to preserve your estate from tax erosion in both Canada and the United States, you may want to consider "insuring" your tax liability. However, you need to be aware of the American "incidents of ownership" rules regarding personally held life insurance. Done incorrectly, your insurance proceeds could be included in your worldwide estate for U.S. estate calculation purposes and end up being taxed as well! Generally, we recommend that life insurance acquired to cover your estate tax exposure be owned through an ILIT (an irrevocable life insurance trust or "wealth replacement" trust) or some form of ownership other than personal ownership. Additional complications come with setting up an ILIT, so we recommend that competent Canada-U.S. counsel be sought beforehand. This is definitely not a "do it yourself" project.

Generally, the U.S. term "incidents of ownership" refers to the rights and economic benefits that an individual derives from a life insurance policy. Under U.S. tax laws, life insurance proceeds are included in the calculation of an individual's worldwide estate if the decedent has any of the following:

• the right to change beneficiaries or their shares,
• the right to surrender the policy for cash or cancel it,
• the right to borrow against the policy reserve, and
• the right to assign the policy or revoke an assignment.

Rent Rather than Purchase U.S. Vacation Property

Personally held real estate in the United States may create U.S. estate tax exposure and is not eligible for the U.S.$2 million estate threshold limitation provided for under the tax treaty. Furthermore, if you choose to rent out U.S. real estate, you'd have to adhere to American and Canadian income tax filing and compliance requirements, as discussed in Chapter 2.

Hold Property Jointly — But Be Careful!

Often U.S. real estate acquired for personal use may be titled on a joint basis with a spouse or family member. When property is held on this basis (jointly titled with rights of survivorship or JTWROS), upon the death of the first owner title automatically passes by operation of law to the co-owner. The presumption by owners who hold property this way is that only 50% of its value will form part of the U.S. gross estate at the first death. Unfortunately, that isn't the case under American rules.

When property is titled jointly with a spouse — or any other joint owner for that matter — the entire value of the property may be subject to U.S. estate tax unless the surviving joint owner can establish that he or she contributed funds to the purchase price. The presumption of the IRS is that the first spouse to die contributed 100% of the purchase price. Unless the surviving joint owner can establish the amount contributed by the decedent, the entire date-of-death value will be subject to U.S. estate tax. If property is held in sole name of the deceased, then the entire value is subject to estate tax.

For the purchase of U.S. real estate on a joint basis to be effective under U.S. tax laws, each purchaser should use his or her own funds or, if necessary, borrow from the other purchaser with a properly documented loan.

Create Tenancy-in-Common Ownership for Valuation Discounts

When property is held this way, valuation for U.S. estate tax purposes is represented by the undivided fractional interest that you own within the American real estate. Your interest can be transferred to others under your will or during your lifetime as a gift. If the transfer is made as a gift, be aware of the U.S. gift tax rules discussed above. Under U.S. gift and estate tax rules, the transfer of an undivided fractional interest is entitled to an estate valuation discount — for lack of marketability. The discount rates generally acceptable tend to fall within the 20% to 35% range. So, if you were to hold a 35% interest as a tenant-in-common of a property worth U.S.$2 million, your valuation for U.S. estate tax purposes could be U.S.$525,000 (U.S.$2 million x 35% reduced by an assumed 25% discount) as opposed to U.S.$700,000.

Although this may be one of the simplest arrangements when the owners of the property are family members, it can be fraught with problems when family or other owners don't get along or have different objectives with respect to the property. We have seen situations where one family member passed away, with the decedent's interest going to his surviving spouse through his will. Unfortunately, none of the family members got along with the surviving spouse, and a number of unique "family dynamics" occurred as a result. Therefore, a clear understanding between all parties of objectives and intentions regarding the property should be reached before titling any property this way.

Finance U.S. Real Estate Using a Non-Recourse Mortgage

Many Canadian snowbirds acquire U.S. real estate with mortgage financing and automatically assume that the mortgage debt directly reduces the amount of the taxable estate. This is not the case. This is only the case if a *non-recourse* mortgage is used. In that case, the full value of the mortgage can be deducted from the value of your U.S. real estate.

A non-recourse mortgage is a debt for which the borrower has no personal liability. If the borrower defaults, the lender's recourse is the sale of the property or foreclosure. The lender doesn't have the legal ability to pursue the borrower for the debt. For this reason, it may be extremely difficult for you to find U.S. lenders who are willing to lend on a non-recourse basis.

The U.S. regulations are clear: "A deduction is allowed from a decedent's gross estate on the full unpaid amount of a mortgage upon, or of any other indebtedness in respect of, any property of the gross estate, . . . provided the value of the property, *undiminished by the amount of the mortgage or indebtedness*, is included in the value of the gross estate." Some advisors "structure" non-recourse mortgages with trusts or between family members. However, it is our opinion that these kinds of arrangements will be challenged by the IRS as not being "bona fide" mortgages.

There was a case in 2001 that came before the U.S. Tax Court, which ruled against the estate's argument that only the net equity of the U.S. real estate should be included in the non-resident's estate. The court held that because there was a recourse note the full value had to be included.

Now, if you do have a traditional mortgage against your American property, you do get a partial deduction. However, the deduction will be prorated to the value of your U.S. assets relative to your worldwide assets. Bear in mind that, in order to get this deduction, your estate must provide a full disclosure of the value of your worldwide assets on the U.S. estate tax return.

It's been our experience that most traditional lenders in the United States are reluctant to offer non-recourse mortgages. First, American citizens already receive a full estate tax deduction based on the outstanding mortgage balance at death, so it's not something that is often specifically requested by a U.S. borrower. Second, most traditional lenders, to reduce their risk, want the ability to go directly after the borrower, so they are unwilling to offer non-recourse mortgages.

However, at the time of writing and finally recognizing the business opportunity that can be generated by offering these types of mortgages, RBC Centura — owned by the Royal Bank of Canada — has developed a non-recourse mortgage geared toward snowbirds wishing to purchase real estate in the United States and to avoid or mitigate their U.S. estate taxes. RBC's product is a three- or five-year, interest-only, adjustable rate mortgage (ARM) amortized over 30 years. If your credit rating is "excellent," it will loan up to 65% of the value of the property to U.S.$1 million or up to 55% to U.S.$2 million. This type of mortgage will be priced 0.5% higher than a traditional mortgage. At the time of writing, RBC Centura has been approved to offer these mortgages in 44 states.

With this type of mortgage, only the equity (value of property less the non-recourse mortgage balance) is subject to U.S. estate tax. Conceivably, if the value of the property were to increase over time or U.S. estate tax laws were to change, you could refinance the mortgage accordingly. Furthermore, the mortgage proceeds could be invested in assets that generate investment income and possibly be tax deductible on your Canadian income tax return. We encourage you to seek professional advice from a Canada-U.S. advisor when implementing this type of arrangement. Our suspicion is that, given RBC Centura's offering of this type of mortgage product, other traditional and non-traditional lenders might follow suit.

Holding U.S. Property through a Canadian Corporation

Many Canadians sought to avoid U.S. estate taxes on their American vacation properties by having them owned by a "single purpose corporation" (SPC). Such a corporation was generally a Canadian company that owned the vacation property as its only asset. In the early 1980s, Revenue Canada issued rulings stating that, if the entire cost of the property and all operating expenses were incurred by the individual owner (and family), then the CRA wouldn't treat the individual as receiving a shareholder benefit under subsection 15(1) of the Income Tax Act of Canada.

The primary intent of this type of structure was to avoid U.S. estate tax, based on the view that the property belongs to the company, which cannot die, and since the shares of the Canadian company owned by the individual are situated outside the United States they are not subject to U.S. estate tax. However, there were concerns in the United States with this arrangement because, if the individual held the property personally before transferring it to the company and then continued to derive a personal benefit from occupying the property, the IRS could "look through" the corporate structure under IRC 2036 — *Transfers with Retained Life Estate* and/or IRC 2038 — *Revocable Transfers*. This would result in the full value of the property becoming subject to U.S. estate tax.

Additionally, while owning American real estate through a Canadian corporation may avoid the U.S. estate tax, the result may be multiple levels of income taxation. For example, if you were to die owning a corporation that owns appreciated U.S. real estate, Canada would impose a tax on the gain from the deemed disposition of the shares at death (unless the shares are transferred to a surviving Canadian resident spouse or a qualifying spousal trust). A subsequent sale of the property by the corporation would result in an additional American tax liability and a Canadian tax liability. However, the Canadian tax liability could be offset by a foreign tax credit for the U.S. taxes paid. When the corporation is ultimately liquidated, there is Canadian tax on the liquidating dividend to the shareholder.

Generally, the Canadian corporation receives a tax refund for the "refundable dividend tax on hand," which is the Canadian federal tax on the taxable capital gains. Since the Canadian federal tax is partially or fully reduced by foreign tax credits, there will be little if any tax refund to the corporation upon liquidation.

Likely bowing to pressure from the U.S. Department of Treasury/IRS, on June 23, 2004, the CRA announced that its policy with respect to shareholders of SPCs would be withdrawn. This meant that shareholders of SPCs could be assessed shareholder benefits after 2005. Given the policy change, you should look at other alternatives to holding U.S. personal use real estate.

The CRA's existing position won't apply, however, to

- new property acquired by an SPC after December 31, 2004; or
- a person who acquired shares of an SPC after December 31, 2004, unless the acquisition resulted from the death of the individual's spouse or common-law partner.

For arrangements in place on December 31, 2004, the CRA's existing position continues to apply until the earlier of

- the disposition of the U.S.-based real estate by the SPC; and
- a disposition of the shares of the SPC, other than on a transfer of the shares to the shareholder's spouse or common-law partner as a result of the death of the shareholder.

Purchase U.S. Real Estate through a Canadian Resident Discretionary Trust

This strategy works only if several family members intend to occupy the American residential property. It doesn't work for a

Canadian single person contemplating the purchase of U.S. real estate.

Prior to purchasing the property, a family member — let's assume the husband — creates a Canadian resident discretionary trust. The husband contributes enough cash to the trust to purchase the property. In this case, the husband can't enjoy any financial benefits of the trust and affect the enjoyment of any of the beneficiaries. Therefore, the husband can't be a trustee or have what is referred to under U.S. rules as any retained powers of appointment — the right to appoint or give away the property.

The spouse and children may be discretionary beneficiaries of the trust. The husband — while married — may use the property "at the sufferance of his spouse." If the wife predeceases the husband and he wants to continue to use the property, he'll be required to pay fair market rent to the trust for the use of the property.

If the family stays within the guidelines of the trust, no U.S. estate tax would be payable at either spouse's death. The trust would also be subject to the lower 15% U.S. long-term capital gains rate on the sale of the property. Additionally, the initial settlor — the husband — may continue to contribute cash to the trust to cover costs.

Since the trust is considered resident in Canada, it is subject to the 21-year deemed disposition rule.

Purchase U.S. Real Estate through a Canadian Partnership

In some cases, we have found that a number of Canadian tax advisors recommend the use of a Canadian partnership to hold U.S. real estate. Such an entity would be treated as a partnership in Canada but would take an election to be taxed as a corporation for U.S. income and estate tax purposes.

Since the entity is a partnership for Canadian purposes, many potential problems resulting from using a corporate structure are avoided. The partnership structure is beneficial since

- the Canadian shareholder benefit rules wouldn't apply;
- the earnings (rental income, capital gain or investment income) would be considered the partners', and thus the partners wouldn't be subject to the additional tax that occurs when the property is held through a Canadian corporation; and
- if the U.S. property is worth more than $10 million, the Federal Large Corporations Tax (LCT) or provincial capital tax would not apply.

For U.S. tax purposes, the partnership would be treated as a Canadian corporation; any assets held by the partnership won't be subject to U.S. estate tax provided that the partnership is the legal and beneficial owner of the property.

We typically see the husband, wife, and children organizing the partnership to purchase the U.S. real estate. They would contribute their own funds to the partnership in an amount equal to their respective partnership interests. The partnership would then make an election for U.S. income tax purposes to be treated and taxed as a corporation.

Annual U.S. corporate income tax returns to report U.S.-source income must be filed on Form 1120F — *U.S. Income Tax Return of a Foreign Corporation.* Expenses for *personal* use of the property are not deductible. Furthermore, if the property is ultimately sold for a profit, and given that the partnership has elected to be treated as an American corporation, the net income (profit on sale) would be subject to tax at the graduated U.S. corporate income tax rates, which range from 15% on taxable income up to U.S.$50,000 to as high as 39% on taxable income between $100,001 and $335,000 and 35% on taxable income between $335,0001 and $10 million. So, as you can see, the income tax result of selling property held through a Canadian partnership can be far more onerous than other alternatives where the maximum U.S. tax rate would be no greater than 15%.

Finally, if the partners are using the property personally, under specific U.S. tax rules there is always the risk the IRS will "look through" the partnership for estate tax purposes. You'll need to review the legal and annual accounting costs to set up and administer such a structure.

Beware of U.S. Living Trust Seminars

We often receive calls from snowbirds or their Canadian advisors telling us that they or their clients transferred their U.S. property into an American "living trust." Holding assets in a U.S. living or revocable discretionary trust is a common estate planning strategy for American citizens and residents. However, it's generally not an effective strategy for Canadians.

Financial or insurance advisors in the United States present living trust workshops in snowbird communities hoping to use the "estate planning process" as a means to gather assets to invest, to sell life insurance and annuities, and to get fees to coordinate the drafting of these types of trusts. Snowbirds who attend these workshops — there is usually free food, so what the heck! — might be compelled to use these trusts as a means to eliminate probate and save on estate taxes. Problem is you aren't a U.S. resident for income, gift, and estate tax purposes, so the full benefits of these trusts just won't work for you. In fact, from the CRA's perspective, you've just got yourself involved in an "offshore" trust and thus subjected yourself to the onerous non-resident trust rules and potential further tax problems.

Filing a U.S. Non-Resident Estate Tax Return

IRS Form 706 NA — *Estate Tax Return of a Nonresident Not a Citizen of the U.S.* must be filed within nine months after the date of death. The tax return along with all schedules, attachments, and the decedent's will should be mailed to the Internal Revenue Service Center, Cincinnati, OH 45999. Even if the estate doesn't have any U.S. estate tax due, an estate tax return still has to be filed if the estate had American situs assets in excess of U.S.$60,000.

The IRS has up to three years after the return was filed to assess taxes (called the statute of limitations). If the return was never filed or is fraudulent, there is no time limit on the ability of the IRS to assess a tax against the estate and ultimately the executor and beneficiaries. That's why we encourage you to file the tax return as soon as possible and get the clock ticking on the statute of limitations.

Summary Comments

Given the tax treaty changes, the larger U.S. estate exemptions, uncertainty about the future U.S. estate tax environment, and your personal objectives, it's critical that you first calculate the level of estate tax exposure that exists before implementing specific strategies to reduce, defer, or eliminate the estate tax.

If you are working with an advisor, have that person first calculate the level of U.S. non-resident estate tax at your death before implementing any strategy. Again, we have found that in many cases simple planning strategies could have been implemented for clients rather than the expensive and often complicated structures proposed by advisors who couldn't even calculate U.S. estate tax if you asked them. Also be aware that with certain structures you have to abide by their mechanics to prevent the IRS from looking through the structure itself. If you are holding U.S. real estate through a Canadian company, trust, or partnership and using the property personally, there is always the risk that the IRS could disallow the structure under IRC 2036 and/or IRC 2038. Again, don't complicate your life any more than it already is.

Will Planning

Wills are the most basic form of estate planning. In its simplest form, a will is a legal statement of one's wishes about how, when, and to whom the assets will go. Laws concerning wills and the succession of property in general come under provincial and state jurisdiction. Wills are extremely important, and with a proper will you can

- avoid intestacy laws (dying without a will);
- appoint appropriate executor(s), trustee(s), and/or guardian(s);
- mitigate hardship for family members and others;
- minimize tax and other administrative costs at death;
- control the settlement of your estate and ensure a smooth transition of assets; and
- use testamentary trusts.

In most cases, a valid Canadian will is recognized as valid in American courts because they often process Canadian wills. Therefore, if you own a U.S. property, it can likely be properly transferred using a Canadian will. Having a will in Canada and a will in the United States for American property is generally not necessary and can complicate the process of estate distribution.

It's important that you have a valid will that properly addresses your intentions for the distribution and/or management of all your property at your death. This is particularly important when you own assets in different locations.

Will Planning Tips for U.S. Property

To minimize issues at death with respect to U.S. property, consider the following in your will planning and drafting.

- Consider having a separate section in the will that deals with any U.S. property you own.
- Separately list all assets and accounts in Canada and the United States.
- Name a specific person to deal with any U.S. estate planning requirements such as ancillary probate.
- If you are from Quebec and have a will in French, consider

having it translated into English for U.S. court filing purposes.

Probate

Probate is the legal process that your estate generally goes
through at your death. This process occurs if you have a will or
if you die intestate (that's right, a will doesn't avoid probate).
Probate can take a long time to complete; it's not uncommon for
an estate to take many months or even years to go through this
process.

Probate can be very costly as well. The jurisdiction (province
or state) where the assets are located will levy a fee on the assets
that are "probatable" in that jurisdiction. This cost can vary
widely and can be quite expensive. On top of any provincial or
state fees your estate may have, it's not uncommon to engage the
services of lawyers and accountants (and their costs). In some
cases, these fees and costs can be eliminated with proper estate
planning. The probate fees in the most common snowbird states
as a percentage of the probated assets are as follows.

Arizona — 0.1%
California — 4.0%
Florida — 3.0%
Hawaii — 3.0%
Texas — 3.0%

Another important issue is that probate makes your personal
affairs a matter of public record. That is, the public has access to
your will, including what you had, who got what you had and
when, and any debts you had. For those assets that flow through
your will at death, this may leave your family, beneficiaries, or
business relationships with no privacy whatsoever, and it
exposes your estate to more challenges along with those attendant costs and delays.

If you die with property in different jurisdictions (e.g., a province and a state), your estate may have to go through probate in both jurisdictions. The first probate will occur in the province or jurisdiction where you resided at the time of death. The second probate, often referred to as "ancillary probate," will take place in the state or jurisdiction where you held property. Ancillary probate deals only with the property located in that state or jurisdiction.

Powers of Attorney

You may have financial accounts and related affairs in both Canada and the United States. A valid legal document called a power of attorney (POA) can be an excellent planning tool to ensure that the management of your assets and affairs continues in the event of your incapacity or inability while in the United States. With a POA, an individual (grantor) appoints and gives authority to another individual to act on his or her behalf.

Under common law, the relation between the donor and his or her attorney is typically governed by the law of the jurisdiction where the power of attorney was executed. Therefore, if you have property — particularly real estate not jointly owned — in a state, for example, we generally recommend that you execute a separate power of attorney to deal with that property in that jurisdiction.

As you are now aware, spending time in the United States and owning U.S. property can create additional estate planning requirements. It's important you have a conversation with those involved in your estate plan to ensure they understand some of the implications you could face by owning assets in the United States. You should also communicate your wishes and the rationale behind each one. Be sure your family members are comfortable in implementing your plan as per your wishes; if they aren't, select other individuals or professionals.

Additional Tips

- Make sure your Canadian will is up to date before you leave for the United States.
- Make sure your power of attorney is up to date, and if you have U.S. real estate or other assets be sure you have a power of attorney that is valid in the state where your property is located.

6

Help! I've Fallen, and I Can't Get Up

Risk Management for Snowbirds

Provincial Health Care Plans

Beyond the currency and tax concerns that confront you on an annual basis, one of the greatest concerns for most Canadian snowbirds is the risk of an accident or illness while in the United States. We are aware of a situation in which a snowbird was enjoying his daily rollerblade along the pathways of a beachfront in Florida. Unfortunately, he took a terrible fall and sustained a serious head injury. He was hospitalized and couldn't return to Canada because of his injury. This individual did not have extra travel insurance and ended up having to use over U.S.$100,000 of his retirement savings to cover his health care needs in the United States.

The costs of medical care south of the border tend to be significantly higher than those under each province's health care insurance program. Therefore, you could be personally responsible for any differences in cost not provided for by your provincial health care plan. And in some cases health services that you require in the United States might not be covered at all under your provincial health care plan. You do not want to lose access to the comprehensive health care benefits provided in Canada, so it's important that, while you are spending time in the United States, you maintain your eligibility within your provincial health insurance program. Health care programs across Canada are undergoing changes in response to budget cuts, so continue to be aware of your provincial health care program and the out-of-country benefits available to you.

In general, Canadian health care insurance plans provide coverage for basic medical and other health care services and are available to all Canadian residents. The method of paying for health care costs varies from province to province. In some provinces, such as Alberta, residents are required to pay monthly premiums for health care coverage. In other provinces, health care costs are incorporated into the provincial tax system so that residents at the highest end of the income scale pay higher taxes and consequently a larger portion of the health care costs. Many seniors profit from this system since their taxation level is often lower after they reach age 65.

As a general rule, all provinces require you to be present in your province of residence at least 183 days in a calendar year in order to maintain your health insurance coverage. It's also important to recognize that, even though you may be covered by provincial health care plans while you are out of the province or country, such benefits may be severely limited and vary in amount by province.

Provincial health care plans cover only a portion of the medical fees in the United States. Most provinces have put strict limits on the amounts they will pay for Canadians who need medical/hospital care in a foreign country. The maximum often falls far short of the costs, especially in the United States. Provincial health care plans also limit the length of time you can be outside the province and still receive coverage; generally, the length of the visit may not exceed six months in any given calendar year. Changes in coverage by provincial health care plans for health care received outside the province or country have made it increasingly necessary for snowbirds to purchase additional insurance, typically referred to as "travel" insurance.

Choosing a Travel Insurance Policy

Medical fees and costs in the United States are often a great deal higher than they are in Canada (e.g., a person with a fractured arm was hospitalized for five days at a total cost of U.S.$12,000, while the provincial health care plan covered only C$1,000).

As a result of reduced coverage, there has been a boom in the number of companies offering travel insurance and a dramatic increase in the cost of this insurance. Regardless of the cost, you can't afford to travel to the United States without additional health insurance, and you need to make sure that the policy you choose will provide adequate coverage for you.

Compare different policies to find the best coverage available to fit your particular needs. You should check with a reputable insurance company or insurance broker to help you evaluate your needs. Read the policies carefully to determine the restrictions and exclusions that might apply to you. Following is a list of some items to check.

- There may be restrictions relating to medical conditions for which you have received treatment prior to the effective date of coverage. Anything related to such a condition will typically not be covered.
- Many policies have age restrictions or age-related rates. Rates may vary depending on how long the coverage is needed. The assumption is that, the longer you are out of Canada, the more likely you may be to have a claim.
- Can the coverage be extended if you choose or are forced to extend your stay? What is required to extend your visit? What procedure will you have to follow when filing a claim?

- What kind of cancellation policy applies, either on your part or on that of the insurer? Be aware of the upper limit of your coverage. Some policies cover claims only up to $25,000. Even a brief hospitalization in the United States can exceed this limit.
- Does the policy cover the cost of returning you to your province of residence for further treatment or in case of death?
- Do you have coverage available through an employee benefit or retirement benefit package?
- Do you have to pay a deductible? If so, how much?
- Does the policy have a co-payment clause? That is, are you required to pay a certain percentage of the medical expenses as well?
- Will the insurance company pay the physician or hospital directly, or will you have to pay the full amount first and try to recover it from the insurance company yourself?
- Will you be required to get approval from your insurance company *before* receiving medical treatment?
- Can the policy coverage be extended if your travel plans change?
- Does your plan have a toll-free or collect emergency number with a 24-hour hotline to provide assistance or verify coverage at any time?
- What is your insurance company's policy and procedure for dealing with complaints?

Many insurance plans won't provide coverage for medical procedures not considered emergency life-saving procedures. Since you, the doctor, and the insurance company may have differing definitions of an emergency procedure, if possible you should contact the insurance company prior to undergoing any treatment.

Additional medical insurance is available through Blue Cross, motor associations, many major Canadian banks, and private insurance companies. The Canadian Snowbird Association has also developed an out-of-country health insurance package for its members.

You should be prepared for the possibility that you may have to pay for your U.S. medical costs first and then take responsibility for recovering your expenses from the provincial health care system directly. If you have additional travel insurance, you should pursue your insurance company first. In some circumstances, it may be difficult for you to receive medical attention in the United States if you don't have sufficient cash or can't prove that you have adequate medical insurance.

Provincial Out-of-Country Coverage

The following information was obtained directly from the websites of the various provincial plans and was accurate at the time of writing. You should verify out-of-country coverage directly with your respective provincial plan prior to any departure from Canada.

British Columbia

If you are eligible for coverage while temporarily absent from British Columbia, the Medical Service Plan (MSP) will help to pay for unexpected medical services you receive anywhere in the world provided that the services are medically required, rendered by a licensed physician, and normally insured by the MSP. Reimbursement is made in Canadian funds and doesn't exceed the amount payable had the same services been performed in British Columbia. Any excess cost is the responsibility of the beneficiary.

The MSP does not cover the services of health care providers other than physicians (e.g., chiropractors or physical therapists) outside the province. Similarly, PharmaCare doesn't provide coverage for prescription drugs or medical supplies when obtained outside British Columbia.

Also be aware that the Ministry of Health doesn't subsidize fees charged for ambulance service obtained outside British

Columbia. If you require ambulance service while in another province or outside Canada, you will be charged the fees established by the out-of-province ambulance service provider. Fees range from several hundred to several thousand dollars. When purchasing additional out-of-province insurance, you are advised to obtain insurance that will cover emergency transportation while you are away and, if necessary, the cost of transportation back to British Columbia.

The cost of medical care outside Canada can be much higher than the amounts payable by the MSP and extended health care plans. For complete protection, additional medical insurance should be purchased from a private insurance company even if you plan to leave the country for only a day. Check the exclusions and limitations of your private insurance policy carefully to ensure that it meets your needs.

If you have extended health benefits through your employer, you should contact the employer to determine the policy provisions prior to purchasing additional medical insurance.

When you receive medical services outside Canada, you need to claim reimbursement from the MSP using an *Out of Country Claim* form (available from its wesbite). The completed form should be returned along with

- an itemized account, including the dates and details of services performed, and
- either the unpaid bills or the original receipts if the bills have been paid.

Out-of-country claims must be submitted within 90 days of the date of service. In-patient hospital claims (and any associated medical claims) must be submitted within six months of discharge.

Payment for physician services will be issued in Canadian funds only and will be paid at the same rate as if the services were received in British Columbia.

For further specifics on out-of-country coverage, check www.healthservices.gov.bc.ca/msp/infoben/leavingbc.html#outofc.

Alberta

Out-of-country insured physician services are payable at the rate that an Alberta physician would receive on a fee-for-service basis or the amount billed, whichever is less. To be eligible for coverage, hospital services must be provided in an active-treatment general or auxiliary hospital. The maximum amount paid for hospital in-patient care provided outside Canada is c$100 per day, not including the day of discharge. The maximum amount paid for routine hospital out-patient services is c$50 per visit, with a limit of one visit per day.

For further information on out-of-country coverage, go to www.health.gov.ab.ca/ahcip/ahcip_claims.html#outside.

Saskatchewan

If you receive medical services outside Canada, you will usually find the costs much higher than in Saskatchewan. If the costs are higher, you will be responsible for paying the difference between the full amount charged and the amount that Saskatchewan Health pays. For this reason, you should buy additional health insurance if you plan to travel outside Canada.

Saskatchewan Health doesn't cover cancer treatment provided outside Canada unless the services have been approved by the Saskatchewan Cancer Agency.

Saskatchewan Health provides limited coverage for emergency medical care from approved general hospitals outside Canada if the same services would be covered in Saskatchewan. Saskatchewan Health will pay

- up to c$100 per day for in-patient services, and
- up to c$50 for an out-patient hospital visit (it won't pay for more than two visits in any one day).

The health agency will pay for emergency services at their eligible rates, and you don't require prior approval. It won't cover any prescriptions filled outside Canada.

For further specifics on out-of-country coverage, check www.health.gov.sk.ca/ps_coverage_opoc.html.

Manitoba

Manitoba Health will pay for emergency doctors' services outside Canada at a rate equal to what a Manitoba doctor would receive for similar services. Emergency hospital care is paid on an average daily rate established by Manitoba Health. You may be charged more than the amount paid by Manitoba Health for services provided outside Canada, and the amount not covered could be substantial and is your responsibility.

You are required to bring or mail your original bills to the Out-of-Province Claim Section at Manitoba Health within six months of receiving care. If you have made payments on your bills, Manitoba Health requires receipts showing the amounts. If you don't include your receipts, Manitoba Health will pay the hospital or doctor directly.

For further information on out-of-country coverage, go to www.gov.mb.ca/health/mhsip/index.html#drprovince.

Ontario

If you are an Ontario resident with a valid Ontario Health Insurance Plan (OHIP) card, you are entitled to certain benefits when traveling outside Canada; however, since coverage for out-of-country health care services is limited, you should consider purchasing supplementary insurance. If you travel out of country for elective medical services that are available in Ontario and can be planned ahead of time, you are not covered.

For residents traveling outside Canada, OHIP covers only emergency health services in connection with an acute, unexpected condition, illness, disease, or injury that arises outside Canada and requires immediate treatment. OHIP will pay for emergency health services as follows.

- If you receive emergency care from a physician or other OHIP-funded health care provider, OHIP will pay to a maximum what it would have paid had the service been provided in Ontario.
  Emergency in-patient hospital services eligible for OHIP coverage will be paid as follows:
- the amount actually billed to a maximum of C$400 per day for higher-level hospital care rendered in a coronary care unit, an intensive care unit, a neonatal or pediatric special care unit, or an operating room of an eligible hospital or health facility, and
- up to C$200 for any other kind of medical care.
- Emergency out-patient services, with the exception of dialysis, will be paid by OHIP at the same rate as those services rendered in Ontario or C$50 per day, whichever is less, for all out-patient services provided on any given day. Out-of-country dialysis treatment will be paid at a rate of C$210 per day.

OHIP will cover these services only when they are provided in hospitals or licensed health facilities.

For out-of-country in-patient services, the hospital or health care facility must routinely perform both complex medical and complex surgical procedures. For out-patient services, they must routinely perform either medical or surgical services.

If you have purchased supplementary insurance, check with your insurance carrier about how you should submit your bills. Otherwise, it's required that you send your itemized bill to your nearest OHIP office within 12 months of receiving treatment. With the bill, also send

- an original, detailed statement, itemized on a fee-for-service basis;

- your original receipt for payment;
- your name and current Ontario address;
- your health number; and
- a completed *Out of Province/Out of Country Claim* (Form 0951-84).

To avoid delays, don't hold your bills and receipts until you return to Ontario. Mail them to your insurance carrier or the ministry as soon as you receive them.

For further details on out-of-country coverage, check www.health.gov.on.ca/english/public/pub/ohip/travel.html.

Quebec

Residents who leave Quebec temporarily are required to notify the Régie de l'assurance maladie if the time they spend outside Quebec during a calendar year totals 183 days or more. To ensure coverage by the Health Insurance Plan during an absence from Quebec, these persons must contact the Régie before leaving.

Only emergency professional services and hospital services received as a result of a sudden illness or an accident are covered, but the Régie reimburses only part of the cost. Professional service fees covered are those rendered by doctors, dentists, and optometrists as long as the same services are covered in Quebec. The Régie issues reimbursements for professional services at amounts not exceeding Quebec rates, even if the insured person paid more. Hospital services covered are those insured under the Hospital Insurance Plan, specifically services received during a hospital stay or at a hospital out-patient clinic. These services include nursing care, diagnostic services, accommodation in a ward (a room with three or more beds), and prescription drugs administered during hospitalization.

If you are hospitalized and have private insurance, you can request that the invoice be sent to your insurance company, which will then claim the amount reimbursed by the Régie. If you don't have private insurance, you must

- pay for the services you receive;
- keep the originals of your invoices and receipts (credit card payment slips or photocopies of both sides of your cancelled checks showing the name of the hospital or health professional); and
- obtain an operative report from the hospital if you underwent major surgery.

You can then apply to the Régie for a reimbursement of professional services at preset rates, as follows:

- a maximum of c$100 per day for hospitalization, and
- up to c$50 per day for health care received at a hospital outpatient clinic.

For hemodialysis and the required medication, the Régie reimburses up to c$220 per treatment, regardless of whether you were hospitalized.

Some health care services received outside Quebec are not covered by the Health Insurance Plan. If a snowbird doesn't take out private insurance for these services before leaving Quebec, he or she must pay the full cost. Here are a few examples:

- any medical services not covered in Quebec;
- services rendered by a health professional other than a doctor, dentist, or optometrist;
- the cost of a private or semi-private hospital room;
- emergency transportation by ground or air;
- the cost of bringing a person back to Quebec; and
- drugs purchased outside Quebec, even if prescribed by a physician (before leaving Quebec, snowbirds who regularly take prescription drugs can ask their pharmacists whether they can obtain the drugs they will need during their absence).

For further specifics on out-of-country coverage, go to www.ramq.gouv.qc.ca/en/citoyens/assurancemaladie/serv_couv _ext/ext_canada.shtml.

Nova Scotia

If you are a Nova Scotia resident traveling outside Canada for a short period of time, Medical Services Insurance (MSI) will provide coverage for emergency medical services only. Out-of-country in-patient hospitalization as the result of an accident or sudden illness while temporarily absent from Canada is covered in Canadian funds at Nova Scotia rates. The current rate for emergency in-patient services is C$525 per day plus 50% of ancillary fees incurred.

The following services are not covered under the MSI program:

- facility and hospital out-patient charges;
- x-ray, diagnostic tests, and laboratory charges from out-patient, emergency, or private facilities;
- pharmacare and children's dental programs; and
- routine vision analysis.

The balance of an account after payment by the department can be quite large, so it's strongly recommended that any resident traveling out of province purchase travel insurance for the period of absence to cover this balance and other insured services. Ambulance services rendered outside Nova Scotia are not subsidized and are therefore the patient's responsibility.

All claims must be received by the department within six months of the date of discharge from the hospital to be eligible for payment. No claim received after six months will be considered.

For further information on out-of-country coverage, consult www.gov.ns.ca/health/msi/moving_travel.asp#3.

Prince Edward Island

In the event that you require hospital or medical services for an accident or sudden illness while absent from Canada, either you can pay the total cost yourself and then claim reimbursement for the insured amount from the Department of Health, or you can arrange to have the insured amount paid directly by the department. Be sure to obtain a detailed invoice and proof of payment for the services you received, and submit your claim to the department within six months of the date of services.

Services for emergency treatment or sudden illness obtained outside Canada are paid for at PEI rates in Canadian dollars. Residents are cautioned that charges for insured services may be considerably higher outside Canada. Payment for any difference between the fee charged and the department payment is the responsibility of the resident. PEI residents visiting other countries are advised to obtain private medical insurance for the period of absence.

If you are referred by a PEI physician to an out-of-country hospital or physician for a service not available in Canada, you must receive prior approval of the medical director. If approval is granted, all charges for insured medical and hospital services may be paid in full by the department. If you don't obtain prior approval, the department will take no responsibility for the costs incurred.

For further specifics on out-of-country coverage, check www.gov.pe.ca/infopei/onelisting.php3?number=76254.

Newfoundland and Labrador

Newfoundland and Labrador will provide coverage under the Medical Care Plan (MCP) to beneficiaries who are temporarily absent. Coverage under the Hospital Insurance Plan will also be provided; the Department of Health and Community Services can provide more information on the services insured outside Newfoundland and Labrador. Coverage under the Dental Health Plan is not available outside the province.

To ensure that coverage remains intact while you are traveling, obtain an Out-of-Province Coverage Certificate from the MCP. Beneficiaries leaving for vacation purposes may receive an initial certificate for up to 12 months of coverage. The normal four-month residency requirement must be met immediately following their return to Newfoundland and Labrador. Further certificates issued will only provide up to eight months of coverage.

With certain exceptions, claims for insured medical services obtained outside Canada are paid at MCP rates, which Newfoundland and Labrador physicians receive. When the amount billed exceeds the amount payable, payment of the difference is the patient's responsibility. Insured medical services obtained outside Canada that are not available in Newfoundland and Labrador but are available in another province are payable at the rates established by the medical care plan in that province. Again, any amount billed that exceeds the amount payable is the patient's responsibility.

If you plan to have insured medical treatment that you think may not be available in Canada, and if you wish to claim reimbursement of related medical costs through the MCP, you must ask your physician to request prior approval from the MCP before obtaining treatment in another country. By doing so, you'll be aware in advance of the rates at which your medical bills will be reimbursed.

If you are granted prior approval based on the unavailability of the services in Canada, the Medical Care Plan will provide coverage for the services. Payment will be in the currency of the country where the services are received provided that the rates are deemed to be fair and reasonable as determined by the Department of Health and Community Services. Prior approval is mandatory to receive payment at rates higher than those published in the MCP or other provincial physician fee schedules. If a patient opts to travel outside the country for medical service/treatment and prior approval hasn't been granted, payment will be in accordance with the established rates outlined above, and any balance remaining is the responsibility of the patient.

For further details on out-of-country coverage, go to www.health.gov.nl.ca/mcp/html/info_ben.htm#oop.

New Brunswick

New Brunswick Medicare covers only emergency out-of-country physician and hospital services or services for which you have received prior approval. An emergency is related to a specific incident that occurs while you are outside Canada where a delay in the provision of treatment, as for fractures, sutures, and cardiac arrests, would threaten life. Emergency services do not include

- services related to a preexisting condition that requires ongoing monitoring, or
- follow-up visits resulting from an out-of-country emergency (these visits should occur in Canada).

New Brunswick Medicare pays
- c$50 a day for out-patient emergency services, and
- c$100 a day for in-patient services resulting from an emergency admission.

These amounts include most laboratory, radiological, or interpretation fees billed separately from the hospital claim. Out-of-country emergency physicians' fees are paid in Canadian funds at rates equal to what a New Brunswick physician would receive for similar services.

For further details on out-of-country coverage, check www.gnb.ca/0051/index-e.asp.

Property Insurance

If you own a home or condo in the United States, ensure that you have a comprehensive homeowner's policy that covers the replacement cost of your U.S. property due to damage from a variety of sources. The policy should also cover risks such as theft, vandalism, and liability. If you are staying in a rental property while in the United States, consider acquiring rental insurance to cover theft and vandalism of your personal property kept in the rental home.

Before spending time in the United States, confirm that your Canadian home insurance policy has a "freezing peril" clause because of the extensive damage that can be caused when water pipes break. Another peril that should be considered is "snow load." Some policies may exclude any protection from damages resulting from excessive snow load on the roof of a home. Most policies stipulate that, when you are away, someone must check your home on a regular basis. You should contact your insurance agent to determine the exclusions in your policy and how you can best deal with them. Your insurance agent should also be able to tell you what arrangements you'll need to make while you are away.

Canadian insurance companies may also have restrictions on the amount of automobile coverage they will extend while you are out of the province or country. Don't assume that your regular insurance policy will provide coverage while you are in the United States. Prior to leaving Canada, check with your insurance agent about your policy coverage and benefits south of the border.

7

Mayday! Mayday!

Finding Help

Having read this book, you may feel like crying out "Mayday!" (*"M'aidez!"* if you're from Quebec). Indeed, you may be feeling overwhelmed with all the things to consider while adopting a temporary lifestyle in the United States. This feeling should provide you with the motivation to address these issues but not to panic. Although limited, help is available. You have to decide what you are going to do and where you need the assistance. Some folks want more help and others less. We encourage you to determine this upfront since it will help to guide you in the relationship you are seeking. Your next step is to go out and find the help you want. This chapter will outline some of the things you need to consider in your search for a competent and qualified Canada-U.S. advisor.

Selecting a Qualified Canada-U.S. Advisor

Today, it seems, everyone is calling himself or herself a "financial planner" or "advisor." In our opinion, no industry has so pillaged a term and created so much confusion as the financial services industry and the term "financial planner." Any relationship has trust as its underpinning. This trust requires a strict upholding of the fiduciary standard to you (versus a suitability standard). The word *fiduciary* is defined as "of or relating to a holding of something in trust for another." This means your interests are put ahead of those of the financial advisors. With a suitability standard, the product or advice simply needs to be suitable to you (leaving lots of room for the recommender to serve his or her own needs), not necessarily the best thing for you. Essentially, the financial product or solution salesperson doesn't have to disclose that he is recommending a particular financial product or solution because he has a quota to meet, a bonus for selling it, or a contest to win — it just has to be suitable. Do you see the chasm between these two standards?

Our firm believes the best way to fulfill the fiduciary responsibility to you is to be fee-only (no product sales, no commissions, payment only from you, the client). The planning process should start by having a conversation about you and what you are trying to achieve, not about a particular product, your investments, or a tax-saving strategy that "fits" into your situation. From there, our role is that of a quarterback to coordinate the bevy of attorneys, insurance agents, accountants, investment managers, and other professionals to ensure that your best interests are served at all times. The key is to focus everyone on the achievement of your goals and objectives. As a result, your Canadian investment advisor's interests or your Canadian accountant's preferences should come secondary to your needs when adopting a temporary lifestyle in the United States.

Competence

The first step in hiring any Canada-U.S. financial advisor is to look for the Registered Financial Planner designation in Canada and the Certified Financial Planner™ designation in Canada and/or the United States. The license to use the RFP® designation is issued by the Institute of Advanced Financial Planners in Canada. The CFP® designation is issued annually by the Certified Financial Planner Board of Standards in the United States and the Financial Planners Standards Council in Canada. To hold these designations, one must complete course requirements and a comprehensive exam. In addition, there are work experience requirements (three years) that must be obtained in the financial services industry before use of the designation will be granted. Maintaining these designations requires meeting ongoing continuing education standards to ensure the licensee is current with the changing rules and regulations. Most important, however, is the requirement to abide by a strict code of ethics. An undergraduate degree and a graduate degree (preferably on both sides of the border) should be considered an asset as well as the Tax and Estate Practitioner (TEP) designation given by the Society of Trust and Estate Practitioners (STEP).

If possible, seek an advisor who is qualified to assist you with your U.S. income tax issues before the U.S. Internal Revenue Service. Such an individual is referred to as an Enrolled Agent (EA). The EA designation is only granted to tax experts directly by the IRS. An individual must complete a rigorous background check and four grueling examinations over a two-day period — the same as a CPA in the United States — to obtain the EA designation. Fewer than a third pass the exams in any year, which cover taxation of individuals, trusts and estates, corporations and partnerships, and ethics. An EA is a representative of the taxpayer — not of the IRS. EAs are allowed to practice before the IRS with the same authority and client privilege as any attorney or CPA. They are the only tax experts granted this authority under U.S. federal law and number fewer than 35,000 in the United States.

The next thing to look at is the experience of the Canada-U.S. advisor you are considering. You need to ask potential advisors if they work on a consistent basis in the Canada-U.S. planning arena. Some people call themselves "cross-border" planners, but under further probing it comes to light that they attended a conference on cross-border planning issues or that the bulk of their clients have no U.S. issues at all. Ask if they have clients who either spend time in the United States or own property there. There is nothing like having someone with the practical experience of working with clients in this unique area. We have seen the negative side of so-called experts, and it ends up costing you twice (a good example is tax preparation: you pay once for the initial work and again to adjust or amend your return to bring you into compliance with the CRA, the IRS, or state taxing authorities), plus there is usually little recourse for a job poorly done. When it comes to qualified Canada-U.S. advisors, be careful you are getting what you pay for!

Unfortunately, there is no formal professional training in Canada-U.S. planning. It has to come with practical experience, "on-the-job" education, and a comprehensive network of professionals. This means that competent Canada-U.S. advisors are in very short supply, and there are only a handful of people who can calculate U.S. non-resident estate tax, prepare U.S. income and estate tax returns, or competently write a comprehensive financial plan addressing both Canadian and American income tax, estate, and financial planning issues. It often comes down to knowing which questions to ask and how to get effective answers. In addition, there are many potential "gray" areas to consider when acquiring U.S. real estate, and often the judgment and experience of a qualified Canada-U.S. advisor are worth more than the fees paid. In the tax preparation arena, there is a greater number of people who can competently deal with Canada-U.S. tax issues and how the treaty between the two countries applies. As always, we recommend you choose professionals carefully and demand full disclosure of their compensation.

The Planning Process

Although this book deals specifically with the financial, tax, and estate planning considerations of Canadians who temporarily spend time or own assets in the United States, our firm focuses on the comprehensive financial planning needs of individuals with Canadian and U.S. interests and assets. That being said, the next thing to focus on when seeking a Canada-U.S. advisor is the process the advisor will follow in developing your financial plan. Lack of a well-defined process is typically indicative of a poor planning approach and, subsequently, poor results. Our years of experience in Canada-U.S. financial planning have led to a very defined process that has proven itself successful many times. As a result, we don't try to alter or find a shortcut around our process. There are too many small details in any Canada-U.S. plan that can create havoc with your unique financial and tax situation. When considering Canada-U.S. advisors, ask if they have a planning process. If so, is it designed to address Canada-U.S. issues specifically? Does the process focus on you and what you are trying to achieve, or does it seem to be promoting a particular product, tax structure, or investment scheme? Any Canada-U.S. plan starts with a thorough exercise setting goals and objectives. This is time consuming but necessary to establish the context in which to place individual Canada-U.S. financial decisions. Ask how much time will be spent understanding your needs and your unique financial situation and how the conversations will be documented. In our experience, this process typically requires two meetings of two to three hours each to fully understand your situation.

Once the process has been outlined, you need to ask if a custom-tailored, written report will be issued. Ask to see a sample Canada-U.S. plan. It's important to note the difference between myriad colored charts produced by most planning, insurance, or investment software and a financial plan containing a detailed analysis of every aspect of your individual financial situation. Be sure that specific recommendations will be given on all aspects outlined above, from cash management and income taxes to Canada-U.S. areas in estate planning.

Client Relationship

Another important consideration when selecting advisors is whether you can work with them or not. Ensure that they know whom they are going to serve (you!). Ask if you'll be working directly with a principal of the firm or with an associate. If an associate, how does the company assign one to you? Is it random, or is there a personality assessment to find the best fit in the firm? Has the associate ever been to Canada or the United States? You'd be surprised how many planners we know who try to advise on U.S. issues from Canada have never even been to the United States and vice versa. How long have they been focusing on Canada-U.S. planning? When you call in, who will take your call? Is this person technically competent, or does he have to ask someone more senior for every answer? Do you share a common heritage? If not, you'll find that the "associate" will typically be your "parrot" to someone senior in the firm who really knows the answers, and this can be a frustrating, time-consuming process for you. Is this person fun to work with? Can you work with this person, and is she a "fit" with the way you like to work (in person, via e-mail, etc.)? You should also know, once your plan is complete, who is going to assist you with implementing it and how much that will cost. Be sure you have a detailed understanding of the recommendations being made, the pros and cons of each, and how each will be implemented. Overall, your specific planning requirements shouldn't be a laborious task, and your consultations should offer healthy interactions that any good relationship is expected to provide.

Nature of the Firm

It's prudent to ask some difficult questions about the firm you are considering. For example, ask about the number of clients lost and gained in the past couple of years. If you get an answer at all, you should ask why people are leaving the firm to glean further insights into your potential relationship with it. If there have been many new clients, you should ask if the firm is on a big marketing push, for you may be lost in the shuffle.

Another difficult question to ask is whether there has been a high rate of employee turnover. If so, it's difficult to retain someone who has an intimate understanding of you and your financial situation, because new "associates" constantly need to be brought up to speed (usually by you because the partners are too busy). A lack of consistency in the relationship can lead to mistakes. Also, if there is significant turnover, you need to ask yourself "Why isn't this firm able to keep its top employees?" Are its hiring practices suspect? Is it just desperate to staff up to handle its marketing growth?

Find out the strategic direction of the firm and what it is trying to achieve; you will gain insights into the motivation of a relationship with you (are you just a fee, or does the company want to help you build a better life?). If there is no limit to its growth, this may indicate a focus on fees rather than on a relationship with you. Get some details about the principals of the firm, such as their ages and retirement/succession plans and so on. Look for principals who are committed to their business over the long term and certainly for as long as you intend to have a relationship with them. You should ask for two or three references of clients who have been with the firm (for varying time periods, starting with relatively new to several years) to get a broad perspective on what it's like to work with this firm. How big is the firm, and how many relationships does it currently have? How many relationships does it have per associate? Per principal? The higher the client-associate ratio for relationships, the more difficult it will be to service you. If you visit the firm, is there a sense of organization or chaos? Ask to see the office of the person you will be working with. Are there files stacked all over the floor, desk, and shelves, or is everything relatively clean and in order? A chaotic firm can mean little or no time to service your needs and one focused on fees rather than clients.

Another area to consider is the agreement you will sign with the prospective firm. Ask for a sample agreement, and be sure you understand the details. Is the agreement long and complicated, with the fee buried deep in the agreement or not present at all? Do you understand how the fee is calculated for your situation? Is this an objective or subjective process? Does the fee seem reasonable for services rendered, and how does it compare with other fee quotes? You should also watch for agreements that lock you in for a defined period of time or levy penalties if you want out before the expiration of your agreement. This is all good for the advisor and bad for you. Why would you want to be cemented in a relationship that isn't working? Why can't the advisor earn your business and keep it voluntarily rather than force you into a contractual relationship? Does the financial planner get all or most of your money up front and therefore leave little incentive to continue servicing you afterward? Ask for an estimated completion date for your financial plan. Asking some pointed questions will ensure you have an advisor you can trust to uphold the fiduciary responsibility to you.

Regulatory Compliance

By law, anyone rendering financial advice must be registered with the appropriate government authority. In the United States, this means your advisor must be registered with the Securities and Exchange Commission or with the appropriate authority in the state where he or she lives. In Canada, any advisor must be registered with the appropriate provincial authority. In the United States, you should ask for a Form ADV disclosure statement, which is required by the regulator and must be provided at your first inquiry about the firm's services. This document must be updated and filed annually, and it contains everything about the financial advisory firm you are considering, including the backgrounds of the professionals employed, the services offered, and how they are compensated. You will also be able to check for any disciplinary hearings or other issues that may be important to you. If you have interests in Canada and the United States, it likely would make the most sense to consider a firm that has offices in both countries that can work together to coordinate your unique planning requirements.

You should also check with industry regulators and associations for more information on the firm you are considering. Most of this can be done online with the Securities and Exchange Commission (www.adviserinfo.sec.gov/), the National Association of Securities Dealers (www.nasd.com), and the local state securities regulator. Also confirm the license to use the CFP® designation at the CFP Board of Standards in the United States (www.cfp-board.org) and the Financial Planners Standards Council (www.cfp-ca.org) in Canada or the Institute of Advanced Financial Planners (www.iafp.ca), which governs the Registered Financial Planner (RFP) designation in Canada. You can also check the background of the licensee, how long she has held the license, and if there have been any disciplinary hearings (and the outcome). Another thing to consider is the advisor's involvement in professional associations. They are a good source of information on the person you are considering to become your trusted financial advisor. In Canada, Advocis (www.advocis.ca) is the largest financial planning organization, and in the United States the equivalent is the Financial Planning Association (www.fpanet.org). There is also the National Association of Personal Financial Advisors (www.feeonly.org), where you can check membership, involvement, standing, and so on.

Compensation

Another important thing you should know is how your advisor is compensated. This is a controversial subject in our industry, so our intent here is to arm you with the information you need so you can make an informed decision and pick the most appropriate compensation structure for your situation. Whether they tell you or not, all financial advisors get paid . . . nobody works for free. There are basically four methods of compensation.

- *Commission only:* the person gets paid commissions and trailers from financial products sold to you; this is the most common method of compensation in the industry and is evidenced by a focus on your investments and the disclaimer that the advisor can't offer tax advice.
- *Fee-offset:* advice is rendered for a fee, but if you purchase a financial product afterward the commissions or trailers are reduced by the fee you have paid up front.
- *Fee-based:* this is a combination of a fixed fee for advice rendered and then commissions and trailers for any products sold to you. In our opinion, it's really "double-dipping," and it's telling how the financial plan typically recommends products on which the person will earn a commission as well.
- *Fee-only:* you pay a fee for advice rendered, and there is no other source of third-party compensation (no commissions, trailers, etc.), similar to how you work today with an accountant or attorney.

Let us say here that our firm is a fee-only financial planning firm, and therefore we are disclosing our bias toward fee-only planning. We believe this method of compensation removes as many conflicts of interest as possible from the relationship with you and puts any firm on your side in rendering advice in your best interests (upholding the fiduciary responsibility to you). When compensation comes from the sale of financial products to you, it creates an inherent conflict of interest because there is generally a quota to meet or a contest to win. Unfortunately, this is perfectly legal in our society because of two very different standards for financial product salespeople versus true financial advisors. In the case of financial product sales, there is a suitability standard, which means the product has to be suitable to your situation in order to avoid the ire of the regulator.

With a fiduciary standard, the regulator requires your interests to come ahead of your advisor's, which means the advice rendered should be as conflict free as possible. We suggest you demand full disclosure and ensure you understand, in dollar terms, how much it will cost to implement any recommendations provided. You should carefully discern between

- *a financial product salesperson,* who renders advice about a particular product;
- *a financial planner,* who renders advice on specific technical topics such as tax or investments;
- *a financial advisor,* who renders comprehensive financial advice based on an understanding of your entire financial situation and what you are trying to achieve; the focus is on you and your financial goals, not on a particular financial product, technical area, or strategy; and
- *a Canada-U.S. advisor,* a financial advisor who specializes in your unique and specific planning requirements, such as a move to the United States, the purchase or sale of U.S. assets, or the estate planning around American assets you may hold at your death.

We have provided a checklist in Appendix C you can use to help you determine exactly what type of advisor you need. It has been our experience that a financial advisor well versed personally and professionally in Canadian and U.S. tax, estate, and financial planning matters is typically the best person to assist you. It really takes a comprehensive understanding of both sides of the border and continual practice in this area to render the best advice to you.

To save a few dollars, some people believe their Canadian chartered account (CA) and their U.S. certified public accountant (CPA) are all they need to address their Canada-U.S. tax needs. We have seen Canadian CAs do things for Canadian tax or liability protection purposes with no idea of the consequences in the United States. Double or even triple taxation has been the result when that person acquired or sold assets in the United States. We have seen U.S. CPAS prepare tax returns with no understanding of IRS or Canada Revenue Agency (CRA) compliance issues. When the first piece of "hate mail" arrives from the IRS or CRA and is presented to the "cross-border tax professional," suddenly calls are no longer returned, or the response "We don't deal with U.S. tax issues" is given.

In terms of attempting to reduce U.S. non-resident estate tax on U.S. real estate, we often hear of Canadian advisors recommending to their clients that they just add another family member to the title of the property as a means to reduce the overall ownership percentage or to ensure that the asset is not subject to probate at death. However, what might seem like a simple solution to a problem only leads to much bigger problems! There is likely a U.S. gift tax return that would need to be filed in this situation. Canadian tax would likely exist too given that the gift would be considered a "deemed sale" for Canadian income tax purposes. Does this meet the client's overall estate planning objectives? We often hear that the intentions of the parents who own a property are to benefit their children equally. However, many times we see that only one child might be included as joint owner of the property. Given how jointly held property passes under the law, this could compromise the estate planning objectives of the family.

We have also seen many situations where U.S. property has been sold by Canadians who were ignorant of the 10% withholding tax requirement under FIRPTA where the net capital gain — or loss in some cases — was well below the 10% withholding tax rate. These individuals were then stuck for more than 18 months waiting for their refund!

Furthermore, we often meet clients who have a complicated, expensive, and administratively burdensome structure to hold their U.S. real estate. Unfortunately, if the advisor had simply "run" the numbers, the tax treaty changes (use of the additional marital tax credit and foreign tax credits at death) would have been sufficient to reduce or eliminate any U.S. estate tax exposure.

Unfortunately, these people are rendering advice in an area they may not be capable of practicing in . . . a clear violation of principle three of the CFP® Code of Ethics and Professional Responsibility (if they hold the CFP® at all). These folks may be welcome on a well-rounded Canada-U.S. planning team, but they require a quarterback to coordinate the activities and to ensure that all the right questions are being asked, and answered, along the way. Failure to put in place a well-thought-out plan, unique to your individual situation, and have it coordinated effectively can have many unintended consequences and cause you no end of grief.

Our Firm

Transition Financial Advisors and Transition Financial Advisors Group Canada ULC use the tagline "Pathways to the U.S." and "Pathways to Canada" to clarify that we specialize in helping people with tax, estate, and financial planning issues in both Canada and the United States. To that end, our firm operates best as a "financial coordinator," the quarterback of your Canada-U.S. planning team. Not only does our firm have the educational background to meet your needs (Brian and I hold both Canadian and American financial planning designations), but we also have the personal experience with our own moves and lifestyles on each side of the border. One of the most important things our firm brings to any relationship is empathy with you in the many joys and frustrations you will experience in snowbirding in the United States. Why? Because we have walked in the shoes you are about to put on. In addition, we share a common Canadian heritage and can easily talk about hockey, Canadian politics, or fishing in Alberta. Brian and I enjoy many relationships with other professionals across Canada and the United States who are competent in Canada-U.S. planning matters and can be brought onto the team as needed. These people include accountants, attorneys, insurance agents, and government contacts. We have chosen this approach over bringing everything in house so we can select the best people to work with you on your Canada-U.S. issues. For example, there may be a competent accountant closer to you who will make it more convenient to prepare your taxes. Why should you have to deal with a firm with limited locations?

Our planning fees are typically based on a sliding scale of your net worth. This approach falls in line with our comprehensive financial planning philosophy because our firm looks at everything related to your temporary move. This may include rendering advice on the income and estate tax implications of acquiring U.S. real estate or providing advice on the homeowner's insurance policy that you will require on the property. Our fee is made known up front and put into an agreement that both you and we sign. The fee is then fixed until the engagement is fulfilled, giving you peace of mind that there are no hidden fees or expenses to surprise you later. Obviously, this is how we feed our families, so we don't render advice for free! When we do have time, we are committed to helping our community through pro bono work, so any work we do for free is done in this area only (budget counseling, teaching, etc.).

In our experience, folks who meet the following criteria will benefit the most from our services:

- desire a close, long-term working relationship versus just a transaction;
- willing to delegate financial matters and have done so in the past;
- believe in our comprehensive planning approach and willing to follow our proven process;
- willing and able to expediently implement the plan (with our assistance) once completed;
- make friends easily and willing to share of themselves, expecting the same in return;

- comfortable using the Internet; and
- have a net worth of $2 million or more.

You can contact us for a no-obligation review of your situation and the opportunities and obstacles your unique financial situation presents. Just go to our website under the "Get Started" tab to download our "Introductory FactFinder." Fill it out to the best of your ability and send it to us. We will contact you to set up an appointment, and with your FactFinder in hand we can be in a better position to discuss your unique situation.

Head Office

Transition Financial Advisors, Inc. — Pathways to the U.S.
Gilbert, AZ
Phone: 480-722-9414
E-mail: book@transitionfinancial.com
www.transitionfinancial.com

Satellite Offices

Transition Financial Advisors Group Canada ULC
Calgary, AB
Miami, FL

Appendix A

Snowbird Resources and
Relevant Websites

- Canadian Snowbird Association — www.snowbirds.org/
- Canadian Passport — www.ppt.gc.ca
- Canadian Consular Affairs — www.voyage.gc.ca
- Canada-U.S. Border Crossing Wait Times —
  www.cbsa-asfc.gc.ca/general/times/menu-e.html
- Canada Revenue Agency — www.ccra-adrc.gc.ca/
- Canada Border Services Agency — www.cbsa-asfc.gc.ca/
- Provincial Health Care Links —
  www.hc-sc.gc.ca/hcs-sss/medi-assur/pt-plans/index_e.html
- Human Resources and Skill Development Canada —
  www.hrsdc.gc.ca/en/home.shtml
- Investment Dealers Association of Canada —
  www.ida.ca/index.html
- Investment Funds Institute of Canada — www.ific.ca

- U.S. Citizenship and Immigration Service —
  www.uscis.gov/graphics/index.htm
- U.S. Customs and Border Protection —
  www.customs.ustreas.gov/xp/cgov/home.xml
- U.S. Internal Revenue Service — www.irs.gov
- Universal Currency Converter — www.xe.com/ucc
- IRS: U.S. Tax Information for Visitors to the United States —
  www.irs.gov/pub/irs-pdf/p519.pdf
- CRA: Canadian Residents Going Down South —
  www.cra-arc.gc.ca/E/pub/tg/p151/p151-e.html
- IRS Form 8840 — *Closer Connection Exception Statement for
  Aliens* — www.irs.gov/pub/irs-pdf/f8840.pdf
- IRS Form 8288 — *U.S. Withholding Tax Return for Disposi-
  tions by Foreign Persons of U.S. Real Property Interests* —
  www.irs.gov/pub/irs-pdf/f8288.pdf
- IRS Form 8288B — *Application for Withholding Certificate for
  Dispositions by Foreign Persons of U.S. Real Property Interests*
  — www.irs.gov/pub/irs-pdf/f8288b.pdf
- IRS Form W-7 — *Application for IRS Individual Tax Identifica-
  tion Number* — www.irs.gov/pub/irs-pdf/fw7.pdf
- IRS Form 1040NR — *U.S. Nonresident Alien Income Tax
  Return* — www.irs.gov/pub/irs-pdf/f1040nr.pdf
- IRS Form 1040NR — *U.S. Nonresident Alien Income Tax
  Return Instructions* — www.irs.gov/pub/irs-pdf/i1040nr.pdf
- IRS Form Schedule D — *Capital Gains and Losses* —
  www.irs.gov/pub/irs-pdf/f1040sd.pdf
- IRS Form Schedule E — *Supplemental Income and Loss* —
  www.irs.gov/pub/irs-pdf/f1040se.pdf

Appendix B

List of Canada–U.S. Border Crossings

This list has been compiled from information on wikipedia.org.

British Columbia/Washington
- 56th Street, Tsawwassen, BC / 56th Street, Point Roberts, WA
- BC Provincial Highway 99, Surrey, BC / Interstate 5, Blaine, WA
- BC Provincial Highway 15, Surrey, BC / State Route 543, Blaine, WA
- 264th Street, Aldergrove, BC / Washington State Route 539, Lynden, WA
- Cherry Street, Huntingdon, BC (Abbotsford) / Cherry Street, Sumas, WA

British Columbia/Idaho
- BC Provincial Highway 9, Kingsgate, BC / U.S. Highway 95/5, Eastport, ID

British Columbia/Montana

- BC Provincial Highway 93, Roosville, BC / U.S. Highway 93, Roosville, MT

Alberta/Montana

- Alberta Provincial Highway 6, Chief Mountain, AB / Montana State Highway 17, Chief Mountain, MT
- Alberta Provincial Highway 2, Carway, AB / U.S. Highway 89, Piegan, MT
- Alberta Provincial Highway 62, Del Bonita, AB / Montana Secondary Highway 213, Del Bonita, MT
- Alberta Provincial Highway 4, Coutts, AB / Interstate 15, Sweetgrass, MT
- Alberta Secondary Highway 880, Aden, AB / Montana Secondary Highway 409, Whitlash, MT
- Alberta Provincial Highway 41, Wild Horse, AB / Montana Secondary Highway 232, Wild Horse, MT

Saskatchewan/Montana

- Saskatchewan Provincial Highway 21, Willow Creek, SK / Montana Secondary Highway 233, Willow Creek, MT
- Saskatchewan Provincial Highway 37, Climax, SK / Montana Secondary Highway 241, Turner, MT
- Saskatchewan Provincial Highway 4, Monchy, SK / Montana State Highway 191, Morgan, MT
- Saskatchewan Provincial Highway 2, Poplar River, SK / Montana State Highway 24, Opheim, MT
- Saskatchewan Provincial Highway 36, Coronach, SK / Montana State Highway 13, Scobey, MT
- Saskatchewan Provincial Highway 34, Beaver, SK / Montana Secondary Highway 511, Whitetail, MT
- Saskatchewan Provincial Highway 6, Regway, SK / Montana State Highway 16, Raymond, MT

Saskatchewan/North Dakota
- North Portal, SK / Portal, ND

Manitoba/North Dakota
- Manitoba Provincial Highway 75, Emerson, MB / North Dakota Interstate 29, Pembina, ND
- Has at least 12 crossings, many with no communities nearby

Ontario/Minnesota
- Ontario Provincial Highway 11, Rainy River, ON / Route 72, Baudette, MN
- Ontario Provincial Highway 71, Fort Frances, ON / Route 53/Route 71, International Falls, MN
- Ontario Provincial Highway 61, Thunder Bay, ON / Minnesota State Highway 61, Grand Portage, MN

Ontario/Michigan
- Sault Ste. Marie International Bridge, Sault Ste. Marie, ON / Sault Ste. Marie, MI
- Blue Water Bridge, Sarnia, ON / Port Huron, MI
- St. Clair Tunnel (railroad)
- Detroit-Windsor Tunnel, Windsor, ON / Interstate 375/Michigan State Highway 10, Detroit, MI
- Michigan Central Railroad Tunnel, Windsor, ON / Detroit, MI
- Ambassador Bridge, Windsor, ON / Detroit, MI

Ontario/New York
- Peace Bridge, Fort Erie, ON / Buffalo, NY
- Rainbow Bridge, Niagara Falls, ON / Niagara Falls, NY
- Whirlpool Rapids Bridge, Niagara Falls, ON / Niagara Falls, NY
- Queenston-Lewiston Bridge, Queenston, ON / Lewiston, NY
- Thousand Islands Bridge, Hill Island, ON / Wellesley Island, NY
- Ogdensburg-Prescott International Bridge, Johnstown, ON / Ogdensburg, NY
- Seaway International Bridge, Cornwall, ON / Massena, NY

Quebec/New York

- Route 132, Dundee, QC / Water Street, Fort Covington, NY
- Route 138, Godmanchester, QC / Route 30, Trout River, NY
- Chemin Jamieson, Elgin, QC / Route 29, North Burke, NY
- Route 202, Hinchinbrooke, QC / Route 52, NY
- Rennie Sideroad, Hinchinbrooke, QC / Earlville Road, Earlville, NY
- Montee Clinton, Franklin, QC / Frontier Road, NY
- Montee Tremblay/Route 209, QC / Route 189, Clinton, NY
- Route 203, Havelock, QC / Cannon Corners Road, NY
- Route 219, Hemmingford, QC / Route 22 (Hemmingford Road), Mooers, NY
- Chemin Ridge/Route 15, St Bernard de Lacolle, QC / Interstate 87, Champlain, NY
- Route 221, St Bernard de Lacolle, QC / Route 276, NY
- Route 223, St Bernard de Lacolle, QC / Route 11, Rouses Point, NY

Quebec/Vermont

- Route 225, QC / Route 225, VT
- Route 133, Saint-Armand, QC / Interstate 89, Highgate Springs, VT
- Route 235, QC / Morses Line, VT
- Route 237, Frelighsburg, QC / Route 108, East Franklin, VT
- Route 139, Abercorn, QC / Route 139, Richford, VT
- Route 243, Potton, QC / Route 243, North Troy, VT
- Route 143, Stanstead, QC / Route 5, Derby Line, VT
- Route 55, Stanstead, QC / Interstate 91, Derby Line, VT
- Route 147, Stanhope, QC / Route 147, Norton, VT
- Route 141, Saint-Herménégilde, QC / Route 141, Canaan, VT
- Route 253, QC / Route 253, Canaan, VT

Quebec/New Hampshire

- Route 257, Chartierville, QC / Route 3, NH

Quebec/Maine

- Route 161, QC / Route 27, ME
- Route 173, Saint-Théophile, QC / Route 201, Sandy Bay Mountain, ME

New Brunswick/Maine

- Clair-Fort Kent Bridge / Clair, NB / Fort Kent, ME
- Edmundston, NB / Madawaska, ME
- Saint Leonard, NB / Van Buren, ME (bridge)
- Route 218, NB / Boundary Road, ME
- Route 375, NB / Route 229, ME
- Route 190, NB / Route 167, ME
- Route 110, Centreville, NB / Boundary Line Road, Bridgewater, ME
- Route 95, Richmond Corner, NB / Interstate 95, Houlton, ME
- Route 122, NB / Boundary Road, ME
- Forest City Road, NB / Forest City Road, ME
- St. Croix, NB / Vanceboro, ME (bridge)
- Mohannes, NB / Woodland, ME (railroad bridge)
- Upper Mills, NB / Baring Plantation, ME (railroad bridge)
- Milltown, NB / Calais, ME (bridge)
- St. Stephen, NB / Calais, ME (bridge)
- Roosevelt Campobello International Bridge

Appendix C

Canada-U.S. Advisor Interview Checklist

Competence

1. Do you hold professional and accredited financial planning designations in Canada and the United States?
2. What other designations, degrees, or training do you have in Canada-U.S. planning?
3. How long have you been practicing specifically in the area of Canada-U.S. planning?
4. How long have you been working at the firm? What is your next career step in the firm?
5. What percentage of your clients are Canada-U.S. clients versus others?
6. Tell me about your own personal experiences in Canada and the United States.

Planning Process

1. Describe in detail the planning process you have to address my Canada-U.S. needs.
2. How do you determine my goals and objectives with respect to my needs?
3. How do you integrate my goals and objectives into a specific plan?
4. Do you have a written sample plan I can review?

Client Relationship

1. Tell me about your firm. How long have you been in business? Please provide me with your Form ADV or other regulatory disclosures.
2. How many employees do you have? How many clients per employee? Per principal?
3. What are your assets or net worth under management?
4. Will I be working directly with a principal or an associate? Why?
5. How do you determine the person I will be working with in the firm?
6. How much employee turnover have you had in the past two years? Why?
7. What is your typical client? What is his or her net worth?
8. What are the principals' goals and objectives for the firm in the next five to 10 years?
9. How old are the principals? What are their plans for retirement and succession? When will that take place?
10. What personalities work best with you? Your firm? Why?
11. How many clients have left the firm over the past two years? Why?
12. How many clients have you gained in the past two years? Why?
13. Where do you custody investment accounts? Why? Are there any conflicts of interest I need to be aware of?
14. What are your personal interests?

Compensation

1. How are you paid? When are you paid?
2. How do you calculate your fees? What is my fee in dollars? Specifically, show me the calculations for my fee.
3. How do you ensure that your fiduciary responsibility to me is given the highest priority?
4. Can I see a sample agreement? How long does my agreement last? How can I terminate it?

Professional Affiliations and Associations

You can consult with the following professional organizations to confirm any credentials or affiliations for the transition planner you have interviewed.

1. *Financial Planners Standards Council:* the organization that licenses and governs the Canadian CFP designation (www.cfp-ca.org/plannersearch/plannersearch.asp, or you can call 1-800-305-9886).

2. *CFP Board of Standards:* the organization that licenses and governs the CFP® designation in the United States (www.cfp.net/search/, or call 1-888-237-6275).

3. *Institute of Advanced Financial Planners:* the organization that licenses and governs the use of the RFP designation in Canada (www.iafp.ca/, or you can call 1-888-298-3292).

4. *U.S. Securities and Exchange Commission:* this is the regulatory body in the United States that governs financial advisors (www.adviserinfo.sec.gov/).

5. *National Association of Personal Financial Advisors:* the only organization in the United States and Canada comprised of fee-only financial advisors (www.fee-only.org, or call 1-800-366-2732).

6. *Financial Planning Association:* the largest association of financial planners in the United States (www.plannersearch.org, or call 1-800-647-6340).

7. *Advocis:* the largest association of financial planners in Canada
(www.advocis.ca/content/find-ad-form.aspx,
or call 1-800-563-5822).

8. *Society of Trust and Estate Practitioners:* the global organization
for those practicing advanced trust and estate matters
(http://www.step.org/searchuser.pl?n=1000).

Appendix D

Canada-U.S. Differences

We've included this information based on our experiences having lived both temporary and permanent lifestyles in each country. We hope that you find this information useful and fun!

Food

One of the biggest adjustments we had to make in moving to the United States was the difference in food between the two countries. Yes, we said food. What do we mean? Here are some of our favorites that we have had to learn to do without because these items are hard to find in the United States.

- Perogies — although we have found them occasionally at Trader Joe's
- Butter tarts and crumpets
- Ginger beef — thin strips, coated with a sweet sauce

- Pancake mix — Mrs. Nunweiler's or Coyote brand (nice and hearty!)
- Snacks — all Old Dutch potato chips, Popcorn Twists, Hostess Hickory Sticks and Shoestrings, Hawkins Cheezies
- Chocolate bars — Jersey Milk, Eat More, Caramilk, Coffee Crisp, Aero, Smarties, Mirage, Wunderbar, Cadbury Bars, Oh Henry!, Glosettes, Maltesers, Crispy Crunch, Crunchie, Big Turk, Mr. Big, Mack Toffee, Malted Milk, Neilson (Coconut Fingers, Golden Buds, Macarons, Slowpokes, Willocrisp), Bridge Mixture, Cherry Blossoms
- Cookies — Dare (Wagon Wheels, Chocolate Fudge, Coffee Break), Christie (Fudgeeo's, Maple Leaf), Dad's (Oatmeal, Oatmeal Chocolate Chip, Oatmeal Raisin)
- Candy/gum — Thrills, Maynard's Wine Gums
- Sauces/syrups/spreads — Roger's Golden syrup, Summerland Sweets syrups, HP Sauce, E.D. Smith Lemon Spread, Shirriff Carmel Spread, Imperial Cinnamon Spread
- Cereals — Post Shreddies, Muesli, Red River, Sunny Boy, Quaker Harvest Crunch
- Beverages — Tim Hortons coffee, Red Rose tea, Mott's Clamato juice, Sun-Rype juice, and of course almost all Canadian beers!
- 222's pain reliever

It is interesting that other Canadians in the United States have noticed they can't find these items, so they have set up websites that can ship these items to you. Check our website at www.transitionfinancial.com for links to some of these companies.

Some other differences we have found or been told about.

- Fruitcake is considered a delicacy in Canada and is found in most wedding cakes and during the Christmas SSN. In the United States, it is considered a social faux pas to give or receive fruitcake.

- You can't find Nanaimo bars anywhere!
- Dairy Queen Brazier in Canada is far better than in the United States.
- Dairy Queen ice milk soft serve is creamier tasting in Canada than in the United States.
- McDonald's offers muffins in Canada, while breakfast burritos are available in the United States.
- KFC is crispier and better tasting in Canada than in the United States.
- KFC gravy is much more flavorful in Canada than in the United States (fries with gravy are uncommon).
- Tim Hortons is available primarily in the border states.
- Earls is starting to open some restaurants in the United States (Scottsdale, AZ, and Lone Tree, CO).
- Boston Pizza has a lot of restaurants in the United States now.
- The Keg is starting to open some restaurants in the United States (AZ, CO, TX, WA).

Here is a list of items we can't find in Canada when we visit up there.

- Poore Brothers potato chips
- Chocolate bars — Hershey's milk chocolate, Almond Joy, Mounds, Baby Ruth, Three Musketeers, Payday, 100 Grand, Milk Duds, Mr. Goodbar
- Malt-O-Meal cereal
- Krispy Kreme donuts (much harder to find)
- Aleve pain reliever

However, here are some things we and others have noted when up in Canada.

- P.F. Chang's Chinese Bistro (Pei Wei is the take out) is

nowhere to be found.

- Ruth's Chris' Steakhouse is absent except for a location in Toronto.
- Good Mexican food and good barbecue are hard to find.
- Portion sizes are generally bigger in the United States, and eating out is cheaper (before the exchange rate).
- The number of restaurants that offer buffet service all day is much greater in the United States than we have found in Canada.
- The selection in most grocery and retail stores is far greater in the United States than in Canada.
- Most "sin" taxes are higher in Canada than in the United States (liquor, wine, beer, cigarettes, cigars, chewing tobacco, gasoline).

If you have something to add to this list, please e-mail us at book@transitionfinancial.com and tell us about it.

The Postal System

- It is a postal code in Canada and a zip code in the United States.
- A first-class stamp costs 42¢ in the United States versus 52¢ in Canada in 2007.
- Mailing a postcard costs 27¢ in the United States versus 52¢ in Canada.
- First-class postage for a regular #10 envelope from the United States to Canada costs 66¢ (est.) versus 93¢ from Canada to the United States.
- It takes approximately 7-10 calendar days for first-class mail to reach Canada from the United States, but it takes approximately 10-14 days for mail in Canada to reach the United States.
- In the United States, a letter mailed for delivery in the same city will typically be delivered the next day, whereas in Canada it can be two to three business days.
- In the United States, mail is delivered on Saturdays. Not so in

Canada.

• If you have friends or relatives in Canada who are mailing out wedding invitations to you in the United States, tell them a U.S. stamp is required for the return postage. Putting a Canadian stamp on a return envelope that originates in the United States is not recognized by the U.S. postal system (however, such letters have been known to slip by).

The English Language

The American version of English is different from the British version used in Canada, so words such as cheque, labour, harbour, centre, and litre become check, labor, harbor, center, and liter. That is why your computer's spell checker may highlight these words as misspelled. The table below shows other differences in the way Canadians use the English language versus Americans.

Canadian versus American English

Canada	U.S.
Pop	Soda or Cokes
Caesar	Bloody Mary
Barbecue	Cookout
Housecoat	Robe
Chesterfield	Sofa/couch
Car accident	Car wreck
Holidays	Vacation
Ensuite	Master bath
Icing Sugar	Powdered Sugar
Cubby Hole	Glove Box
Penitentiary	Prison
Donair	Gyro
Supper	Dinner
Felts	Markers
Chocolate bar	Candy bar
Garbage	Trash

Canada	U.S. cont'd
Buns	Rolls
Thongs	Flip flops
Slacks	Pants
Runners	Tennis shoes/Sneakers
Golf shirt	Polo shirt
Squares	Dessert
Garburator	Garbage disposal
Washroom	Restroom
Marks	Grades
Junior high	Middle school
University	College
Floating rate	Adjustable rate
Cutlery	Silverware
Pot holders	Hot pads
Tea towels	Wash towels
Porridge	Oatmeal
Toque	Toboggan hat
Brown bread	Wheat bread
Sucker	Lollipop
Soother	Pacifier
Licken	Spanking
Standard	Stick shift
Needle	Shot
Slippers	House shoes
Guaranteed investment certificate (GIC)	Certificate of deposit (CD)

The Metric System

After you have been in the United States for a while, you'll start talking in terms of gallons, Fahrenheit, et cetera. However, when you are talking with your friends and family back home in Canada, they will be talking in terms of liters, Celsius, et cetera. The following should help you in these conversations.

- Celsius can be converted to Fahrenheit quickly by doubling the Celsius number and adding 30 (e.g., 30°C x 2 = 60 + 30 = approximately 90°F). For negative numbers, the calculation works like this: -30°C x 2 = -60 + 30 = approximately -30°F.
- If you want an exact conversion, use (°F / 32) x 5/9 = °C.
- The boiling point is 212°F versus 100°C.
- Freezing occurs at -32°F versus 0°C.
- Room temperature is 70°F versus 20°C.
- Body temperature is 98.6°F versus 37°C.
- Mr. Fahrenheit was the only glass blower in his day who could blow a symmetrical, thin cylinder (thermometer) to record temperatures. He set -32°F as his starting point because it was the lowest temperature he could record with his device.
- 100 km/hr = approximately 60 mph.
- 1 mile = 1.61 km or 1 km = 0.62 mile.
- 1 inch = 2.54 centimeters.
- 1 meter = 3.28 feet.
- The United States adheres to the metric system for track and field, while Canada uses yards for football.
- 1 liter = 1.06 quarts.
- 1 ton = 1.1 tonnes (pronounced "tawns").
- 1 imperial gallon = 4.5 liters.
- 1 U.S. gallon = 3.8 liters.
- 1 imperial gallon = 0.84 U.S. gallon.
- 1 kilogram = 2.2 pounds.
- 500 grams = 1.1 pounds.

Geography

- The Russian Federation is the largest country in the world, Canada is second, China is third, the United States is fourth, and Brazil is fifth.
- Canada covers 3,849,674 square miles (9,970,610 square km), of which 291,576 square miles (755,180 square km) are inland water (7.6%), while the United States covers 3,717,811 square

miles (9,629,091 square km), of which 181,519 square miles (470,131 square km) are inland water (4.9%).

- Quebec is the largest province, and Ontario is second, while Alaska is the largest state, and Texas is second (note: the Yukon, Northwest Territories, and Nunavat are territories, not provinces).
- Texas is 13,314 square miles larger than Alberta.
- The population of Canada is about the same as the population of California (about 32.6 million). The population of the United States crossed 300 million in October of 2006 (approximately 10 times that of Canada).
- The largest metropolitan populations in the United States are New York with approximately 20 million and Los Angeles at approximately 15 million. In Canada, Toronto has approximately 4.3 million, and Montreal has approximately 3.3 million.
- Canada shares a 5,527 mile (8,895 km) border with the United States spanning 12 states and is the largest unprotected border in the world.
- The lowest temperature ever recorded in Canada was -81° F (-63° C) in Snag, Yukon, while the highest was 115° F (46° C) at Gleichen, Alberta.

Government

- In the United States, Congress creates the laws governing the land (legislative branch) and is made up of the Senate and the House of Representatives. In Canada, the Parliament is made up of the Senate (upper house), the House of Commons (lower house), and the Sovereign (represented by the governor general).
- Canada is a constitutional monarchy under the queen, while the United States is an independent republic.
- Canada has a parliamentary-cabinet government versus a presidential-congressional government in the United States. This means that in the United States the president is both the

head of state and the head of government. In Canada, the queen (represented by the governor general) is the head of state, while the prime minister is the head of government.

- The Republicans (the GOP, for Grand Old Party — the elephant) are most akin to the Conservatives in Canada (the Tories).
- The Democrats (whose symbol is the donkey) are akin to the Liberals (Grits) in Canada.
- It is a governor who heads the state government in the United States, while in Canada it is a premier who heads the provincial government.
- The Canadian equivalent to the CIA (Central Intelligence Agency) in the United States is CSIS (Canadian Security Intelligence Service).
- The Canada Pension Plan can be collected as early as age 60, whereas U.S. Social Security can be collected as early as age 62.
- Canada is part of the British Commonwealth (along with Australia, New Zealand, and India, among other countries), while the United States is not.
- Unlike in Canada, U.S. health care coverage (Medicare) does not start until age 65; for those under this age, it is available for the indigent through Medicaid. Many people receive health insurance as a benefit from their employers, but if you are self-employed or a part-time worker you have to "go bare" or obtain coverage on your own.
- There are 11 statutory holidays in both Canada and the United States. In the latter country, Thanksgiving is on the last Thursday in November versus the second Monday in October in Canada; Memorial Day in the United States is the fourth Monday of May versus Remembrance Day in Canada on November 11th; Victoria Day in Canada is the third Monday of May; while Independence Day in the United States is July 4 versus Canada Day on July 1. There is no holiday for Good Friday or Boxing Day in the United States.

Miscellaneous Trivia

- Both Saskatchewan and Arizona do not change their clocks for daylight savings time.
- U.S. banks typically do not offer currency exchange services, unlike Canadian banks.
- Canadian banks charge a fee for each check, while most U.S. banks offer free checking.
- Americans refer to grades 7 and 8 as middle school, while in Canada grades 7, 8, and 9 are known as junior high.
- American high school is grades 9, 10, 11, and 12; the grades are referred to in collegiate fashion as freshman, sophomore, junior, and senior.
- In NFL football, the field is 100 yards long, and the game has four downs, while the CFL field is 110 yards long, and the game has three downs.
- Winnie the Pooh and the telephone were both created in Canada.

The Tax System

- Tax-filing deadlines are April 15th in the United States and April 30th in Canada for personal taxes.
- In Canada, you get a Social Insurance Number (SIN), while in the United States you get a Social Security Number (SSN).
- One return is filed per married couple in the United States versus one return per person in Canada.
- A W2 slip in the United States is equivalent to a T4 slip in Canada.
- A 1099-INT or 1099-DIV slip is generally equivalent to a T3 or T5 slip in Canada.
- In Canada, only Quebec has a separate return and collects its own taxes. In the United States, 43 states have separate returns and collect their own taxes (the other seven do not have state income taxes).
- Both Canada and the United States allow a tax deduction for medical expenses but limit it by 3% of net income and 7.5%

of adjusted gross income respectively.

- The closest thing to an RRSP in the United States is an Individual Retirement Account (IRA); unlike the IRA, RRSP contributions are always deductible.

- In Canada, lottery winnings are not taxable and are paid out in a lump sum. In the United States, lottery winnings are taxable and are paid out over a 20-year period unless the cash option is requested in advance.

- Both tax systems have an alternative minimum tax.

Index